14.03

A Teacher's Guide to
MULTICULTURAL EDUCATION

Basil Blackwell

Copyright © Jon Nixon 1985

First published 1985
Reprinted 1986, 1987

Basil Blackwell Ltd
108 Cowley Road, Oxford OX4 1JF, UK

Basil Blackwell Inc.
432 Park Avenue South, Suite 1503
New York, NY 10016, USA

British Library Cataloguing in Publication Data

Nixon, Jon
    A teacher's guide to multicultural education.
    1. Children of minorities – Education –
    Great Britain
    I. Title
    371.97′0941   LC3736.G

    ISBN 0–631–13561–8
    ISBN 0–631–13983–4 Pbk

Library of Congress Cataloging in Publication Data

Nixon, Jon
    A teacher's guide to multicultural education.
    Bibliography: p. 170
    Includes index.
    1. Intercultural education – United States. 2. Home
    and school – United States.   I. Title.
    LC1099.N59   1985   370.19′6   84–19136

    ISBN 0–631–13561–8
    ISBN 0–631–13983–4 (pbk.)

Typeset by Cambrian Typesetters,
Frimley, Camberley, Surrey
Printed in Great Britain by
Billing and Sons Ltd, Worcester

Contents

Preface and Acknowledgements

This book is based on four assumptions:

1 that racism is primarily a *system* of domination and oppression and may, therefore, be a matter of result rather than intent;
2 that schools have participated, and continue to participate in this discriminatory system;
3 that teachers can, with difficulty, counter the institutional racism within their own places of work through planned research and development; and
4 that, in order to do so, they require support from the institutions in which they work and from the wider educational context.

In working out the implications of these assumptions I have relied heavily on the responses of those practising teachers who, between 1981 and 1984, were members of the Education for a Multicultural Society Option and the Applied Research Honours Module of the In-Service B.Ed. degree course at Middlesex Polytechnic, neither of which is now in operation. I would like to thank them for the open dialogue achieved during our seminar sessions. In addition I would like to record my thanks to those numerous teachers, parents and administrators up and down the country with whom I have talked, either formally or informally, about the issues raised in this book.

Elyse Dodgson discussed with me many of the structures and arguments as I was formulating them. Ernald Nixon suggested stylistic changes to the final draft. I am indebted to both. Any factual inaccuracies or limitations in the range of reference are, of course, my own responsibility.

Jon Nixon

Note

I have used the term 'black' throughout this book to refer to people of South Asian, African and Afro-Caribbean origin. This term should not be taken to imply a cultural homogeneity among the various groups to which it refers. Occasionally, the term 'New Commonwealth' is used to refer to the Commonwealth countries excluding the 'Old Commonwealth', i.e. Australia, New Zealand and Canada, and to Pakistan which left the Commonwealth in 1972.

There was this Englishman who worked in the London office of a multinational corporation based in the United States. He drove home one evening in his Japanese car. His wife, who worked in a firm which imported German kitchen equipment, was already at home. Her small Italian car was often quicker through the traffic. After a meal which included New Zealand lamb, Californian carrots, Mexican honey, French cheese and Spanish wine, they settled down to watch a programme on their television set, which had been made in Finland. The programme was a retrospective celebration of the war to recapture the Falkland Islands. As they watched it they felt warmly patriotic, and very proud to be British.

Raymond Williams

CHAPTER ONE

The Scope of the Task

The debate about multicultural education is a lively one, with widely divergent views strongly held and often vigorously expressed. In this and the following chapter I shall highlight some of the key issues in the debate with a view to defining the more creative and, as yet, emergent elements within it. The practices of schooling, I shall argue, should be reconstructed around a serious and prolonged consideration of the principle of equality and the implications of this principle for the education of all pupils in, and for, a multicultural society.

It is all too easy when discussing these implications, however, to ignore the diversity of policy and practice within multicultural education and thereby to limit the scope of its development. Thus multicultural education as a general category is all too often collapsed into one or other of its constituent elements: the special needs of pupils from minority ethnic groups, for example, or the problems and possibilities of teaching in the multiracial classroom. The purpose of this chapter is to broaden the terms of reference so that, in later chapters, the various elements that comprise multicultural education can be distinguished and seen as parts of a coordinated whole-school programme.

Whom, then, should we be educating for a multicultural society? In what areas does multicultural education have relevance? To what aspects of schooling does it relate? The scope of our task is defined throughout this chapter in terms of a response to these questions. What is offered is not an abstract definition for armchair theorists but a programme of action for practitioners located at precise points and within specific sectors of the school system.

EDUCATION FOR ALL

The earliest attempts in this country to prepare pupils for life in a multicultural society took the form of 'black studies' courses. One of the most successful of these was the one mounted at Tulse Hill, south London, during the early 1970s. It arose from discussions among some members of staff and senior pupils early in 1971. A sixth-form course was considered most appropriate initially, both because the pupils wanted this and because it was relatively easy to introduce a new course within the existing general studies arrangements. The course began with a consideration of the situation in Brixton and in this country as a whole at that time. This was followed by looking into the past for the causes of black immigration to Britain and so to a study of the history and cultures of the Caribbean, Africa, Asia and South America.

Tulse Hill was not the only pioneering school, however. The Social Studies department at William Penn School, again in south London, also developed a 'black studies' syllabus. This was designed to cover a two-year course and was aimed mainly at children of West Indian origin. The course adopted a historical approach progressing from the beginning of modern colonialism in the sixteenth century, through the situation of the black slaves in the West Indian plantations, to the post-colonial situation in the ex-colonies and the economic and social circumstances of immigrants in Britain.

Underpinning this syllabus was the notion of 'compensation'. Morris Pollack, Head of Social Studies at William Penn School, in his preamble to the syllabus claimed that the purpose of any 'black studies' course is to provide: 'a means of compensating for inadequacies of understanding, lack of identity and poor self-image, sheer ignorance, the holding of myths and prejudices, feelings of superiority and hostility so that a degree of understanding and humility may lead to mutual respect' (Pollack, 1972, 10). The assumption here is that the black child is in certain crucial respects culturally deprived and that this deprivation can be countered by a quick rewrite of the history books. It is an assumption we shall be exploring in more detail in the following chapter. For the purposes of the present argument suffice to say that during the early 1970s the emphasis within what is now generally referred to as multicultural education was unequivocally upon the black child.

The irony of this particular emphasis was quickly spotted. Racism was seen to be a problem which in this country was, to a very large extent, created and fostered by the white population. If anyone was in need of compensatory education it was, therefore, the white child. It was very largely in recognition of this fact that the staff of Tulse Hill School in September 1972 extended their work in this area by introducing topics and themes based on Africa and the Caribbean into the first and second year integrated studies course. As Bev Woodroffe, who was at that time Head of English at Tulse Hill, pointed out, it was important 'to involve as many pupils as possible of whatever group' (Townsend and Brittan, 1973, 89).

At the national level this insight lay at the heart of one of the very first curriculum research and development projects to confront the issue of racism in the classroom. The Programme of Research in the Problems and Effects of Teaching about Race Relations ran between 1972 and 1975 and sought to involve teachers in exploring racism as an issue with groups of pupils. The project concentrated on three main teaching strategies, the first two of which were funded by the SSRC and the third by the Gulbenkian Foundation: strategy A involved the teacher in the role of neutral chairperson; strategy B involved a non-neutral teacher who felt free to give his or her view and to introduce material in order to promote racial tolerance; and strategy C took the form of improvised drama. Over 40 schools, chosen from both rural and inner-city areas, took part in the project. During the experiment the teachers concentrated on developing the understanding of all their pupils, not just those from ethnic minority groups.

This broadening of focus has characterized much of the developmental work carried out in the field of multicultural education over the last ten years. Those education authorities that have responded to the Race Relations Act of 1976, which obliged them to take positive action to eliminate discrimination and promote equal opportunities, have tended to develop local policies that stress understanding and good relations between all groups in the community. The implications of this response as far as the school curriculum is concerned have been significant and wide-ranging.

They ought not to blind us, however, to the fact that children from ethnic minority groups have certain special needs which require urgent and coordinated attention from all sections of the education service. Clearly, the language needs of those for whom English is a second language are a top priority here, as are the language needs of the West Indian child. The Rampton Report (Department of Education and Science, 1981) highlighted the latter in its discussion of the factors contributing to the underachievement of West Indian children as a group in British schools. Chapter 7 of this book reviews the major issues in the debate and considers practical strategies for the development of an effective language policy in multiracial schools.

Necessary though such a policy is in preparing pupils for life in a multicultural society, it is not in itself sufficient. Indeed, the assumption that multicultural education exists primarily for the benefit of the black child is at best patronizing and could well be seen as an example of what the Rampton Report referred to a 'unintentional racism' (Department of Education and Science, 1981, 12). Multicultural education to be effective must rest on a broader base than that provided by a 'black studies' course or a special language-needs programme. It must focus on the general curriculum needs of all pupils as well as on the special needs of some.

These general curriculum needs apply as much to younger as to older pupils. It is sometimes assumed that younger children are somehow encapsulated from the ethnocentricity of their elders. However, this assumption has been seriously challenged over the last ten years. Christopher Bagley and Bernard Coard (1975) have argued from their study of children in three multiracial schools in London that the self-esteem of children of West Indian origin is impaired at an early age. David Milner, who studied 300 children drawn equally from West Indian, Asian and English groups in two large English cities, also concluded that black British children show a 'strong preference for the dominant white majority group and a tendency to devaluate their own group' (Milner, 1975, 121).

These research findings have recently been criticized by Maureen Stone (1981) who sees West Indian children as the victims, not of their own low self-esteem, but of the low expectations imposed upon them by the state through an inappropriate system of compulsory education. The Rampton

Report located the problem prior to the years of compulsory schooling in the inadequate provision of pre-school services. This inadequacy, the report argued, discriminates against the black British population which, as a group, has a relatively high proportion of young children with working mothers (Department of Education and Science, 1981, 15).

Whether one chooses, like Bagley and Coard (1975) and Milner (1975), to pose the problem in terms of the supposed low self-image of the black child or, like Stone (1981) and Rampton (Department of Education and Science, 1981), in terms of the discrimination practised by the dominant white majority, one thing is sure: pupils in infant and junior schools require specific and urgent preparation for life in a multicultural society. For they too endure the reality of racial inequality. Moreover, if this inequality is eventually to be eradicated, it will be partly through the increased understanding and improved inter-racial attitudes of those who are as yet very young.

This assumption lies behind much of the developmental work carried out within the field of multicultural education throughout the early years of schooling. Sylvia Collicott, an infants teacher in the London Borough of Haringey, provides a useful example of how teachers can create links between the experience of the young child and issues relating to the theme of migration. Working from the idea that 'moving house is part of the human story . . . a consistent theme running through history,' she tried in her own classroom to find ways of helping the pupils to think and talk about why people move from place to place and what it feels like to be on the move:

Why do people from Pakistan come to work in England? Why do people emigrate to Australia? Why do some hill farmers of Afghanistan want to move to Alaska? These may seem far flung concepts from the business of buying one house and selling another, but they are part and parcel of the same theme. Tackle the subject on the basis of the children's own experience, but try to examine the concepts behind, and try to stretch the children to a greater knowledge and understanding. (Collicott, 1980)

The work started with personal reminiscences and shared anecdotes. Plenty of the children could remember moving, or could talk about best friends who had moved away:

The children couldn't stop talking, once they started, not just about the physical act of moving, but their feelings about it. Why do people move house? Tracy's dad had been unemployed in Coventry for some months and had returned to London with his family to find work. Strangely he soon got offered a job in Coventry and had to commute from London! In our conversations, we concluded that some people were happy to move and some were not. People can move willingly or they can be moved against their will. Some of the children also talked about their parents moving to England to get a better life. I suggested that they should ask their parents about their first impressions when they arrived and how they felt about such a big move.

We talked about *how* people move. A furniture van can be hired to carry the heavy furniture. It could be cheaper to move if you knew someone with a van. How would you move furniture if you moved to another country? Some of the children explained to me that their parents came with no furniture, just their suitcases. (ibid.)

Clearly, the value of this work is dependent upon the teacher's ability to build slowly towards the central concepts through anecdote, informal discussion and personal reminiscence. Given a willingness by the teacher to respond to the pupils' own insights and sensitivities and to gather these into an increased understanding of the central concepts, there is no reason why young children should be prevented from tackling themes such as migrant labour. Moreover, with a very general starting point like that of 'moving house', the theme gains relevance for all children regardless of their ethnic background.

Whom, then, should we be educating for life in a multicultural society? The answer, of course, is everyone. For all pupils – regardless of their age and origins – are members of a culturally diverse society. As such, their understanding of that diversity ought to be one of the main aims of any education service which aspires to equip young people with the skills and knowledge necessary for contemporary life.

WHITE AWARENESS

It is hardly surprising that the examples cited so far all refer to work carried out in schools situated in areas of high multiethnic population. For, in Britain, multiracial schools have been the pioneers in the area of multicultural education. Two unfortunate consequences have followed from this state of affairs. First, outside the urban environment the notion of cultural diversity has tended to be dismissed as part of 'the inner-city problem'; and, secondly, both inside and outside the multiracial areas of Britain there has been a failure to recognize the extent to which patterns of cultural diversity differ from community to community. Thus, even when multicultural education has been seen as having relevance for all pupils, it has been very largely restricted, in its development, to the inner city and, in its focus, to a narrow interpretation of the diversity of cultures.

Between September 1972 and March 1973 the Schools Council commissioned the NFER to conduct a short survey with the purpose of investigating teachers' views as to syllabuses and the need for development, and to identify current innovation with regard to multicultural education. The sample of schools used in the survey was composed of multiracial and non-multiracial primary and secondary schools selected from two types of local education authority: those with less than 300 immigrant pupils in January 1971 and those with at least 500 in January 1971. One of the key questions on the survey sent to these schools was: 'Do you foresee any changes in your school's (department's) syllabuses in order to make them more applicable to pupils in a multiracial society?' (Townsend and Brittan, 1973, 47).

Although an encouraging proportion of teachers foresaw changes in their syllabuses, these changes tended to be extensions of work already being carried out rather than radically new departures in terms of either curriculum content or teaching methods. A number of headteachers of non-multiracial schools saw no necessity whatsoever to change syllabuses, as in the following cases:

There has always been a multiracial society in this country. Why should we suddenly start preparing children for it?

I do not consider it the responsibility of an English State School to cater for the development of cultures and customs of a foreign nature.

> We have so few immigrant pupils, and those few present no insurmountable problems. At this school, at this point in time, I cannot see a necessity for any particular structured 'preparation for a multiracial society'.
>
> It is anticipated that there will be a fairly slow increase of immigrants and when every class has a proportion the syllabus will then be reconsidered. (ibid., 13, 15 and 47)

Clearly, many of those working in non-multiracial schools felt that the preparation of pupils for life in a multicultural society lacked relevance to their pupils' situation. Many, indeed, would seem to have held the view that the development of the curriculum along these lines was actually against the interests of their pupils.

One would have hoped that over the last ten years the attitude of those working in non-multiracial schools would have changed significantly. However, this is far from the case. In a recent survey of secondary schools in 70 local education authorities only 25 per cent of schools with a 'low' concentration of minority ethnic groups (i.e. those schools located in areas where less than 2½ per cent of the total number of births are to women from the New Commonwealth) reported that some of their teaching reflected a multicultural society. Moreover, in those schools where developments were being undertaken these were frequently restricted to work in religious studies. Very few schools reported that they had systematically considered the implications of a multicultural society for the curriculum as a whole. As the authors of the research report pointed out, 'major initiatives are necessary if schools in these authorities are to be convinced of the relevance to their teaching of a multi-ethnic society' (Little and Willey, 1981, 30).

This question of relevance can be partially answered by the argument that pupils in non-multiracial schools are still members of a multiracial society and that, as such, they require an education which prepares them for life in such a society. This argument, however, does not fully resolve the problem: it asserts the social relevance of multicultural education without explaining how it can become personally relevant for those in non-multiracial areas. What is needed is a notion of cultural diversity which is applicable to the apparently homogeneous community as well as to its obviously heterogeneous counterpart. Only when multicultural education is guided by such a notion can those in non-multiracial schools be expected to see it as having relevance to their own situation.

A striking example of the way in which schools might begin to work from the diversity of cultures within their own communities can be found in the Integrated Studies course developed by a group of teachers in Derry, Northern Ireland. The aims of the course, which is offered to fourth- and fifth-year pupils at the Boys' Secondary School in Coleraine, are as follows:

1. To allow pupils to focus on problems and issues which have direct relevance to their lives both now and in the future.
2. To allow pupils to discuss controversial issues in an objective manner basing judgement on rationality and the use of valid evidence.
3. To make pupils aware of the valuing process, to encourage them to examine the basis of their own beliefs, values and attitudes and to help them to understand the same of other people, especially those opposed to their own.
4. To help pupils in the skill of organising their own experience and information into more abstract concepts so that they may perform more efficiently on an intellectual level.
5. To help pupils develop their basic skills in literacy.
   (Coleraine Boys' Secondary School, undated)

The course was designed to be topic based; topics being drawn from the subject specialist areas of economics, sociology, political science, geography, history and literature. The core of the teaching in all topics is discussion, although improvised drama is also sometimes used as a means of exploring and recording particular issues.

A number of topics covered on the course are of particular relevance to the present argument. These include: pupil culture, the place of women in society, prejudice and discrimination, and conflict in Northern Ireland. Clearly, the last of these is closely related to the personal experience of each of the pupils in this predominantly Protestant school. However, there is also a serious attempt to ground the other topics in the social reality of the local situation. In exploring prejudice and discrimination, for example, pupils begin by discussing their attitudes to 'Glentoran Fans, Irishmen, Catholics, Inst. Boys, Homosexuals'. Similarly, in discussing the place of women in society, the boys are asked to consider the Equal Pay Act and the Sex Discrimination Act in relation to their own families and communities. The value of this approach, then, is that it allows questions of race, class and gender to be localized and, moreover, that it presents these as interconnected elements within the immediate social context of the pupils.

The term 'multicultural education', as opposed to 'multi-ethnic education' or 'multiracial education', would seem to be particularly appropriate to this venture. For it raises the question of multiple cultural foci, and challenges, by implication if not explicitly, the idea of an integral indigenous culture. It begins to explore, in a situation of great political sensitivity, the nature of 'culture' and its function within that politically sensitive arena.

There is no suggestion here that multicultural education should be limited to an exploration of the cultural diversity within one's own locality. The point to be stressed is that such an exploration may be a useful starting point and is, anyway, of considerable educational value in itself. Nevertheless, a full understanding of our own multicultural society today depends, I believe, upon our willingness to confront the imperialist experience: conquest, subjugation, settlement, annexation, exploitation and slavery. Inevitably, therefore, a study of the cultures and histories of those British people who originate from the New Commonwealth becomes a core element in any attempt to educate pupils for a multicultural society. Moreover, it is in non-multiracial areas that this core element should now be evident; in the curricula of all teacher-training institutions and all schools. A simple, practical example of what this entails was given by a student teacher on teaching practice.

The student in question was involved in a six-week practice in a primary school in a town far away from those areas of Britain that are generally considered to be multiracial. It is highly unlikely that any of the eight- and nine-year-olds in her class had ever spoken at length to anyone whose family had come to this country from Jamaica. Yet it was this West Indian island that the student took as the subject on which most of their work was to be based over the six-week period.

The focus of the project was the history of the people of this island. The children produced their own condensed visual accounts of this history in the form of a strip cartoon, detailing each stage in Jamaica's development, from the Arawak Indians to the present day.

The immediate, visible evidence of the results of this six-week project were, as the student's tutor recorded, impressive in themselves:

> a vividly colourful class painting and collage of a Jamaican market scene filling the whole of one wall; dramatic cut-out silhouettes of human figures linked by chains along another wall; a polished improvised drama presentation by the class of a triangular slave-trading expedition – England – Africa – Jamaica – England; imaginative stories about reacting to a natural disaster . . . written by the children individually; plus, of course, all the other background work contained in the individual project folders. (Commission for Racial Equality, 1980, 3)

Beyond all this, however, the significance of the undertaking in terms of conveying to the children a vivid impression of a living culture whose development has been so closely inter-woven with our own cannot easily be measured.

It is unlikely that this impression would have been anywhere near as vivid had it not been for a further initiative taken by the student teacher. For the single most exciting feature of the whole project was the establishing of contact with a primary school in a rural area of Jamaica. The result was an exchange of letters between the English class and a class of children of equivalent age in the Jamaican school. This strategy ensured that for the English pupils Jamaica was neither a spot on a map nor a section of a history book, but part – however small – of their own experience of cultural exchange.

The patterns of cultural diversity within contemporary society are themselves infinitely diverse. They vary from area to area, school to school, child to child. To impose upon this diversity a crude dichotomy – to see it only in terms of black culture and white culture – would be to reveal a want of judgement, of discernment. Multicultural education ought to be the expression of a heuristic urge to probe behind that dichotomy; to discover that variousness in others and ourselves that is the strength of any multicultural society.

THE WHOLE SCHOOL

Throughout this book the stress is upon the whole environment of learning. Too often the task of preparing pupils for life in a multicultural society has been framed by narrow curricular concerns that have prevented any serious consideration of those influences and forces that are usually referred to as the 'hidden curriculum'. It is this 'hidden curriculum' which informs and shapes all the learning – whether intentional or otherwise – that takes place in schools. Another, perhaps simpler, way of making the same point would be to say that education for a multicultural society is concerned with more than just curriculum content. Styles of teaching, patterns of pastoral care, and the relations between school and parents transmit vital messages to pupils concerning the attitudes, values and priorities of the staff. There is no suggestion here that the review of curriculum content is unimportant, but only that this activity must be placed within the context of whole-school evaluation and development. What is needed is a broad perspectiv which would allow the practitioner to look at how the curriculum finds its way into the classroom and how the concerns of the classroom are in turn reflected in the broad organizational structures of the school.

Over the last decade this more expansive view has begun to prevail as the 'hidden curriculum' has gradually undergone a process of disclosure. This process is, of course, by no means complete. Nevertheless, partly as a result of the pioneering work of the 'new sociologists' throughout the early 1970s (Young, 1971), many teachers have become acutely aware of the extent to which knowledge is socially constructed. This 'interactionist' theory of knowledge is now undoubtedly one of the major intellectual influences upon school policy and practice.

Not surprisingly this shift of emphasis can be traced in the changing pattern of priorities within multicultural education. Early projects in this field tended to be almost exclusively concerned with teaching materials. The ILEA World History Project serves as a useful example in this respect. Set up in 1970 under the Staff Inspector for History and Social Sciences it began largely as a result of the doubt expressed by history teachers concerning the relevance of traditional chronological British history to the multicultural society developing in inner London. The immediate task, therefore, for the two experienced teachers who were seconded to the project full time was to provide learning materials for use in the classroom.

As the project developed, however, this task underwent considerable revision. For as soon as the packs of materials were avilable the demand from teachers was for assistance with their effective use. Discussions began to centre on the implications of introducing the new subject matter into the classroom, and focused on such questions as:

> How could the World History packs and ETV pro-grammes be used in the mixed ability group, as part of a course integrated with other subjects, as a basis for external examinations, in general studies? What were the strengths and weaknesses of the worksheet? Was the adaptable videotape, expensive though it might be for schools, preferred to the live TV programmes? How could teachers assess progress and what was being assessed? (World History Project, 1978, 2)

This particular attempt to render the curriculum responsive to the needs of a multicultural society involved, in other words, not only the inclusion of new areas of study but also, in the long run, the acquisition of new teaching methods and new styles of classroom organization. Slowly the project was edging its way towards the 'hidden curriculum'.

It was this covert territory that was chosen as the site of a later ILEA project set up in 1978. The Lambeth Whole School Project, which covered two secondary schools and four junior and four infant units, sought to identify processes by which schools could review the requirements of their multicultural populations in all aspects of their life and work and develop appropriate responses. The elements of school life involved in the project were:

(1) School organisation and pastoral care;
(2) Language development;
(3) Curriculum;
(4) Development and organisation of resources;
(5) Home and community/school interaction;

(6) Staff development;
(7) In-service training. (Inner London Education Authority, 1978)

Work undertaken in the project schools provided the practical basis for the investigation of these elements.

ILEA is not alone in stressing the need for a whole-school approach to multicultural education. Walsall Education Committee, for example, has come out strongly in support of such an approach:

> If the education service as a whole is to respond to the needs of a multicultural society, a coordinated approach will be necessary for adoption alike by all schools, whether or not they have any pupils from ethnic minority backgrounds. The size of this task cannot be underestimated. Its successful completion depends not on the mere promotion in schools of 'fringe' activities such as Asian dance, steel bands etc. (although these have a part to play in contributing to an awareness of cultural differences) but on the much more fundamental question of ensuring that a multi-ethnic dimension should permeate both the everyday learning experience of all pupils and the thinking of all those responsible for providing those experiences. In other words, what is called for is a re-examination of the curriculum from first principles. (Walsall Metropolitan Borough, 1982)

The process of permeation referred to in this extract will be discussed in more detail in chapter 4. It should be noted at the outset, however, that the task as defined by Walsall Education Committee relies upon the willingness of all those involved in educating pupils for a multicultural society to rethink their own assumptions and to re-examine their own practices.

What this entails becomes clearer on turning to a summary of statements made with regard to the development of multicultural education in the London Borough of Brent and based on submissions from working parties chaired by the local education authority advisers. Included as an appendix to a major report by the Director of Education to the Brent Education Committee in March 1982, this summary includes the following questions:

Is there any explicit school position about overt racialist activities, such as objectionable graffiti, circulation of racist literature, activities of racialist organisations?

Are the terms 'multicultural' and 'ethnic' used as substitute words for Asian, African or Caribbean, or are they used in their strict and true meaning which includes white groups?

Are other terms such as 'nationality' and 'British' used correctly or as substitute words for other things: (Brent London Borough, 1982)

These questions quite clearly imply the need for a firm anti-racist stance by the staff as a whole. They imply also, however, the need for a careful consideration by all teachers of their own attitudes and of how these attitudes are reflected in the language of instruction and interaction. It is not just that teachers need to talk – to one another and to their pupils – about these matters, but that they need to acquire a mode of discourse sufficiently discriminating to make the talk worthwhile.

No such discourse can be achieved solely through the formulation of a checklist of questions, regardless of how comprehensive and meticulous this may be. For a checklist can convey little of the complexity of the relationships existing between the various elements of school life. The diverse aspects of schooling, which may be neatly isolated on paper, become in practice finely meshed. This has serious implications for those who are concerned with understanding what is happening in schools. For it means that there are never any absolutely valid starting points; no problems which are finally and definitely solved. On the contrary, each individual fact or idea assumes its significance only when it takes up its place in the whole, in the same way as the whole can be understood only by our increased knowledge of the partial and incomplete facts which constitute it. The process of understanding is thus to be considered as a perpetual movement to and fro, from the whole to the parts and from the parts back to the whole again; a constant dialogue between means and ends.

This dialogue is more than mere self-reflection. It is what actually takes place between individual teachers, between teachers and parents, and pupils and teachers, when the staff of a school is committed to a serious review of the work of the whole institution. Without this urge towards democratic evaluation and corporate planning no attempt to develop a whole-school policy on multicultural education is likely to prove very effective. Indeed, the impact of such a policy would depend almost entirely upon the quality of the collaboration within the school.

In this chapter I have set out to define the parameters of multicultural education. I have argued that the preparation of pupils for life in a multicultural society has relevance for: (1) all pupils,not just those from ethnic minority groups; (2) all areas, not just those with multiracial populations; and (3) the whole school, not just the formal curriculum. Cultural diversity, I have suggested, is an aspect of everyone's life. For some, however, it can only be experienced as a sharp edge of racial discrimination and prejudice. This is why a recognition of racism ought to be one of the inevitable outcomes of multicultural education. For any study of the pattern of relationships existing between cultural groups within Britain must sooner or later pick out racism as a recurring strand in that pattern. Moreover, those with a specific interest in multicultural education must face the fact that certain policies and practices associated with it have themselves contributed to the history of racial discrimination in post-war Britain. Before multicultural education can be reconstructed as a vital force within British schooling, those elements in its own development which have served to maintain the present state of racial inequality must, therefore, be identified. It is to this theme that we shall now turn.

CHAPTER TWO

A Rationale

All too often multicultural education is presented as an
expression of a single viewpoint: an intellectually coherent
construct, systematic in its practices and consistent in its
policies. Even a superficial glance at its development reveals
the crudity of this presentation. There are in fact deep
differences of opinion among those who firmly believe themselves to be educating pupils for life in a multicultural society.
Moreover, these differences centre, not on purely procedural
matters, but on issues of value which raise socially and
politically significant questions about the purpose of schooling.
This chapter addresses such questions. It sets out to uncover
the rationales implicit in various practices and policies
associated with multicultural education and to make explicit
an alternative rationale based on the concept of equality and
justice.

COMPROMISED BEGINNINGS

Multicultural education developed within an ideological framework which was explicitly assimilationist. No sooner had the
impact of New Commonwealth children on the British school
system been felt in the post-war era (see figure 1), than it was
defined in terms of a threat to existing values. The Commonwealth Immigrants Advisory Council in its 1962/3 Report to
the Home Secretary, while conceding that the children of
parents brought up in another culture should be encouraged to

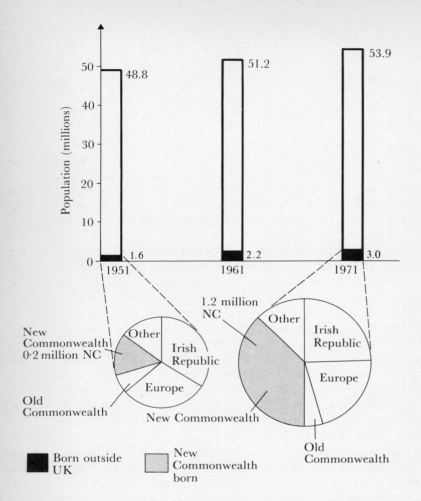

Figure 1 *Resident population of Great Britain by country of birth*

In 1972 1.2 million of the British population had been born in the
New Commonwealth. When the estimated figures for those born
in the New Commonwealth who were white are exluded (0.3 million),
however, and the estimates for those born in Britain who were black
are included (0.5 million), the total black population in 1971 was in
fact 1.4 million (see Runnymede Trust and Radical Statistics Race
Group, 1980, 3).

Source: Office of Population Censuses and Surveys, 1977, table 5.7.

respect it, was adamant that 'a national system cannot be expected to perpetuate the different values of immigrant groups' (Commonwealth Immigrants Advisory Council, 1964, para. 10).

The view was expressed even more unequivocally two years later when, in DES Circular 7/65, the Ministry of Education under Sir Edward Boyle recommended a policy of 'dispersal' (Department of Education and Science, 1965). According to this policy, no school should contain more than 30 per cent immigrant children. Although local authorities slowly phased out their dispersal programmes, which with the exception of the London Borough of Ealing were officially abandoned altogether in 1973, the damage had already been done. The bussing 'solution' was a clear indication of the black community in Britain that local education authorities saw black pupils as a 'problem'.

It was, however, the 'solution' itself which created the real problem. Bussing proved to be a great physical burden and resulted in many black children being deprived of normal childhood. Basically, the policy of 'dispersal' put up to three hours on their working day and on the working day of their mothers and fathers who had to wake them up early and prepare them for school. The distance between home and school meant that parents were unable to take as much interest in their children's schooling as they might have done with a neighbourhood school. The disenchantment of the black community with British schooling can be traced back to the bitterness engendered by Circular 7/65 (ibid.).

The flames of this disenchantment were fanned by the growing concern at the number of West Indian children in Educationally Sub-Normal (ESN) Schools. In August 1970 a three-day seminar was organized by the Caribbean Educationists Association, later to be called the Caribbean Education and Community Workers Association (CECWA). The programme included a paper by Bernard Coard entitled 'The Problems of the West Indian Child in an ESN School'. This paper was redrafted after the conference, and published by CECWA in May 1971 as 'How the West Indian Child is Made Educationally Sub-Normal in the British School System' (Coard, 1971). The response was a publisher's dream. Ten thousand copies were sold.

The legacy of assimilationist thinking is all too apparent in contemporary schooling. It is there, for example, in the well-meaning, if misguided, refusal of many teachers to make a distinction between black pupils and others. The Rampton Report referred to this attitude as the 'colour-blind' approach and stressed that to adopt such a view of children is in effect 'to ignore important differences between them which may give rise to particular educational needs' (Department of Education and Science, 1981, 13). To regard all children as equal, the report maintained, should not mean that they all receive the same educational treatment.

Assimilationist thinking also lurks behind certain attitudes towards language in the classroom. It is still often assumed that before children can possibly learn anything or be integrated into the mainstream of the education system they need to learn to speak 'correct' or 'standard' English. The fallacy of this deficit model is not that it assumes the right of each child to speak 'standard' English – itself an important principle – but that it denies entirely the value of the child's own language usage as a learning medium. This denial is particularly damaging to working-class pupils and to|black pupils, whose non-standard forms may, as William Labov has suggested (Labov, 1973), be highly expressive and capable of communicating great subtlety of argument.

Allied to this view of non-standard English as being in some way deficient is the still widespread belief that all curricula should reflect at all times British traditions, history, customs and culture. Such a belief is sometimes asserted as a point of principle. More often, however, it is presented as a pragmatic response to what are seen as the exigencies of schooling. Thus, we hear the English specialist arguing that, although it may be desirable to study literature drawn from a wide range of cultural traditions, there is just not enough time. Or the history teacher justifies a Eurocentric approach to the subject on the grounds that the public examinations system requires it. Clearly, time is an important factor and public examinations can operate as a constraint upon creative and innovative teaching. But why should the time factor prevent us from introducing pupils, even if only occasionally, to literature produced outside Britain? And why should a syllabus which focuses on British history not be used as an opportunity to include material relating to the history of black people in Britain? (See, for example, File and Power, 1981; Scobie, 1972; and Shyllon, 1974 and 1977.) There are in fact no good reasons unless one assumes that the purpose of education within a multicultural society is to assimilate all pupils into mainstream British culture.

The weaknesses of an educational approach based on this assumption have been summarized succinctly in a discussion paper produced by the Advisory Committee for Multicultural Education operating within Berkshire (this summary has now been adopted, with minor alterations and no acknowledgement, by the ILEA as part of its 'Policy for Equality' (Inner London Education Authority, 1983, 3, 5)):

(1) It defines the black community in schools and society as the 'problem', and therefore not only fails to challenge negative views about black people but also actually promotes and strengthens such views, both in schools and in society.

(2) It places black children at an extremely serious disadvantage, since if they are to succeed in the education system they are required to ignore or disown their own cultural identity and background, and their own and their community's experiences of discrimination and prejudice.

(3) It reflects an inaccurate or inadequate view of Britain's position in world society, both historically and at the present time, and therefore miseducates all children, white as well as black.

(4) It is racist, insofar as it reflects and communicates a notion of white cultural superiority. This is damaging to white children as well as black.

(5) It fails to appreciate that white people have very much to learn from the experience of black people: their struggle against oppression, their movements in daily life between two or more cultures, their achievement as individuals and communities in coping with rapid social and cultural change. (Berkshire Royal County, 1982, 6)

The perspective criticized here in the Berkshire document came under increasing criticism throughout the 1970s. So much so, in fact, that assimilationist assumptions exist today only as residual elements within a changing pedagogy. Nevertheless, they continue to exert a strong influence on teachers' attitudes, on the content of the curriculum, and on the organization of the school as a whole. The notion of assimilation lurks – as a covert rationale – behind many of the policies and practices to which administrators, politicians and teachers still cling.

Although multicultural education is to a large extent a reaction against this covert rationale, it has itself, as we have seen, been implicated in the development of assimilationist policies (such as that of 'dispersal') and of assimilationist practices (such as that of the 'colour-blind' approach). To argue along these lines is not to deny the capacity of multicultural education for change and innovation, but to assert the ideological power of assimilationist thinking in post-war Britain. Multicultural education was, and still is, compromised by its beginnings.

THE PLURALIST DILEMMA

Public reaction to the assimilationist features of the education service highlighted by Bernard Coard (1971) has been anticipated by Roy Jenkins' much quoted definition of integration included in an address delivered in 1966. In it he spoke of integration as 'not a flattering process of assimilation but equal opportunity accompanied by cultural diversity in an atmosphere of mutual tolerance' (Jenkins, 1966). The replacement of the assimilationist perspective with a cultural pluralist perspective heralded a proliferation of courses and conferences for teachers and of advisory posts created to deal with the problem of immigrant education. Multicultural education had come of age.

The pluralist perspective still dominates within multicultural education. From this more progressive vantage point the diversity of contemporary culture is stressed and teachers are encouraged to build on this diversity in the development of curricula sensitive to the needs of a multicultural society. 'The attitude of active pluralism', according to a working party of teachers at Birley High School in Manchester, 'celebrates differences while allowing differences. It deprives neither the "host" community nor the minority groups, but enhances each' (Birley High School, 1980, 1).

The example of Birley High School is worth careful consideration, since it represents a major attempt on behalf of a group of teachers to rethink their educational priorities according to pluralist principles. Working from the assumption that 'contemporary Britain is part of the global village and contains a wide variety of social and ethnic groups' (ibid., 3), the teachers defined the aim of multicultural education as being 'to promote a positive self-image and respect for the attitudes and values of others' (ibid., 2). The major theme running through their summary of recommendations is the need for an awareness and appreciation, by both teachers and pupils alike, of cultural differences:

(1) A positive policy to promote cultural awareness across the whole life of the school should be formulated.
(2) Teachers must be encouraged to learn about the backgrounds and values of the various cultural groups which make up the community and about all the resources available.
(3) The development of social awareness by the pupils must be supported and the links between the school and the community must be developed for their benefit.
(4) School assemblies should give everyone the opportunity to learn about the concepts and values of all faiths and to celebrate and enjoy differences. (ibid., 42)

Clearly, we are faced here with a serious attempt by a group of teachers to review and develop the work of a multiracial school situated in an area with more than its fair share of social and economic problems. It may seem churlish, therefore, to seek to criticize their attempt. However, a number of critiques of the pluralist perspective as adopted by schools such as Birley High School have been developed over the last few years and these deserve some attention; particularly so, since all too often they are mentioned only in order to be dismissed without any detailed discussion (see, for example, Lynch, 1983b, 17).

The critics in question raise important issues about the adequacy of the pluralist perspective and about the relevance of notions such as 'the global village' and 'positive self-image' to the education of pupils for a multicultural society. In particular they argue that multiculturalism as practised in schools is primarily about control. Farrukh Dhondy, for example, while conceding that the impetus that gave rise to the earliest 'black studies' courses in Britain was 'an inspiration to know yourself and feel your power', maintains that the 'co-option of the impulse and the demand killed the interest which black youth took in the "subject" ' (Dhondy, 1982, 50). Chris Mullard's argument is similar. Multicultural education, he writes, 'in its articulated practices is none other than a more sophisticated form of social control which successfully attempts to distort and redefine the reality of racism in schools and society' (Mullard, 1980, 18). The point is made even more succinctly by Hazel Carby: 'The multicultural curriculum was from its inception part of state strategies of social control' (Carby, 1982, 194).

The intellectual and political differences between the various critics of pluralism ought not to be underestimated. On one point, however, they are in broad agreement. For they share a grave mistrust of the principle of 'mutual tolerance' as evoked by Roy Jenkins in 1966. Equality, they argue, cannot be achieved through cultural diversity; it cannot be removed from the realm of politics. To aim at mutual tolerance – whether in the classroom or in society at large – without also aiming at an increased understanding and firm rejection of the existing state of inequality is an attempt at ideological control.

To the concerned teacher working in Birley High School, or wherever, the argument so far may seem to be taking the form of an uncomfortable and frustrating dilemma: either one does nothing and is accused, at the very least, of apathy, or one does something and risks being accused of tokenism. One is either, in the words of the Rampton Report, 'unintentionally racist' (Department of Education and Science, 1981, 12), or, to quote Hazel Carby again, indulging in 'a superficial gesture in an attempt to control the rising level of politicised black conscious-ness' (Carby, 1982, 194). Whichever way one turns one is culpable and the plea of worthy intentions would seem to be disallowed. That is the pluralist dilemma.

This polarization is an unfortunate feature of the debate within multicultural education; unfortunate, because it tends to reduce what ought to be genuine critical discussion to the level of rhetoric and slogan-swopping. One of the now classic formulations of this polarization is that between 'multicultural-ism' and 'anti-racist teaching' (Dodgson and Stewart, 1981). The purpose of constructing such a dichotomy is, presumably, to emphasize the central importance of racism in any discussion of the relation between ethnic groups. Responding to this view a number of teachers have tried to resolve the pluralist dilemma they found themselves in by thinking through the pedagogical implications of introducing into the classroom a discussion of racism.

The following extract from a fifth-year lesson in an all-girls comprehensive school in the London Borough of Haringey may serve as a useful example. The discussion was by way of preparation for an improvisatory drama session based, as the teacher put it, 'on the idea of what it's like to be black in a white community'.

Pupil: Miss, I think once they say 'Get the West Indians out!' they are going to start on the Greeks, the Irish . . .

Pupil: They're trying to get all of them out, all immigrants out.

Pupil: The English always like to have a scapegoat. First it was the Irish that they said were depending on the state. Then it was the Jews. Then they felt sorry for the Jews because everyone else was feeling sorry for the Jews; and then it was the Greeks, and then it was . . . and now its the coloureds. They just need someone. They cannot blame it on themselves.

Teacher: So do you feel, then, that the National Front are getting support because people want a scapegoat?

Pupil: Because they . . . they're going to people and telling them 'Oh, look at him. He's doing better than you. He's foreign. You should be doing that job. He should be doing this.' Or something like that. They're bringing hatred.

Teacher: Because no one can accept failure, and they need someone to blame.

Pupil: And it's easy to blame someone that's not . . .

Teacher: What sort of thing are they worried about, then, the people who support the National Front?

Pupil: They're just worried about getting left behind.

Teacher: As a country do you think?

Pupil: No, they think the ones who are taking over . . .

Pupil: Even if they are taking over, they're not taking

> over by wanting to. It's just that, I dunno, it's
> just that in most important jobs, or really dirty
> industrial jobs that need to be done, it's always
> the foreigners doing them.

Pupil: Yes, that's true.

The lesson in which this discussion took place was documented
as part of the SSRC/Gulbenkian Programme of Research into
the Problems and Effects of Teaching about Race Relations,
based at the Centre for Applied Research in Education,
University of East Anglia, and directed by Lawrence Stenhouse between 1972 and 1975. It is discussed in much greater
detail in the drama case studies produced as part of that
project (Nixon, 1982b, 187–94). For the purposes of the
present argument it is sufficient to point out two characteristic
features of the discussion quoted above: first, it treats racism
as a case of individual prejudice and, secondly, it presents this
prejudice as if it were limited in the main to members of
extremist political groups such as the National Front.

Such discussions, argues Robert Jeffcoate in his book
Positive Image (1979), are particularly valuable to 'white racist
children' who, he claims, 'for the most part need support and
sympathy, not gagging' (ibid., 107):

> Whether teachers like it or not, the school has to find a
> forum of some kind within its walls for the discussion of
> the National Front's ideas and literature once they make
> their presence felt. I would not want to pretend that the
> task will be an easy one. In schools with poor race
> relationships it may prove well nigh impossible. But the
> attempt has to be made, for the school is probably the
> only place in most children's experience where it can be
> undertaken with a semblance of rationality. (ibid., 104)

Writing as one of those who, as he puts it, 'espouse the liberal
ideology', Jeffcoate presents a model of multicultural education
that aims at the celebration of 'international friendship and
understanding' (ibid., 122).

Understanding of this kind, he maintains, depends upon
the existence of an 'open' classroom: ' "open" in its pattern of
communication; and "open" in the relationship between
teacher and learners' (ibid., 117). The case for giving racists a
voice in school is not based entirely on tactical considerations,

therefore. It is also, as far as Jeffcoate is concerned, a matter of principle, of rights. For if children are to decide for themselves where they stand politically and culturally, they need to be protected from the ideological bias of their teachers. They need, in other words, an unthreatening context in which they can explore freely their own prejudices and anxieties.

The major criticism of this approach is that it reduces the issue of racism to a mere matter of individual ignorance. Farrukh Dhondy made exactly this point when dissociating himself from the work of the Programme of Research into the Problems and Effects of Teaching about Race Relations:

> Is the problem of race relations the problem of the prejudice of fellow workers, or is it a problem generated by the socio-economic history of the peoples and classes that were forced to enter the colonial relationship? These are not exclusive alternatives. The answer is that the problem has a socio-economic root and a cultural manifestation. In which case the approach which does not point at the root is heavily biased against the student who is being taught not to be prejudiced. In the course of such teaching, we have to say to the white child: 'You are sick' and this we refuse to do. (Dhondy, 1972)

Racism, then, according to Dhondy, cannot be treated simply as a set of prejudices entertained by extremists. It must also be seen as a form of institutional discrimination in which everyone is implicated.

It would be a pity if the kind of criticism put forward by Dhondy led to a complete rejection of the attempt to discuss racial prejudice with pupils. For there is undoubtedly a relation between institutional racism, which springs from the socio-economic history of colonialism, and racial prejudice, which springs from individual ignorance; a relation which is assumed by Dhondy himself in the passage just quoted. No matter how deeply teachers go into the socio-economic history of racism they need to show that this generates particular interactions between groups of people. Moreover, in showing this they need to explain what students will be most sensitive to; what, in a searching analysis of the pedagogical problems inherent in teaching about race, Stuart Hall has referred to as 'the interplay of feelings . . . structured around the awareness of racial difference' (Hall, 1980, 6).

The attempt to resolve the pluralist dilemma by means of programmes of work in which pupils discuss racism as an issue is not without its problems. Certainly, teachers need to be critical of any rationale which mentions racism solely in terms of personal or interpersonal attitudes. But, equally, they need to be critical of any rationale that drives a wedge between an understanding of the structural features of racism and an understanding of how these features shape our attitudes and feelings, our relationships and values. Racism is neither prejudice nor power; it is what happens when these two couple. Any attempt to progress beyond a mere presentation of cultural diversity and to show the inequality which characterizes the relation between cultures demands a pedagogy that respects both the personal and the political.

THE NOTION OF 'SELF-IMAGE'

The introduction into the classroom of discussions focusing on racism is not the only response to what was referred to above as the pluralist dilemma. A second and equally influential response to the criticism that cultural pluralism fails to confront the inequality between cultures sought to explain this inequality in terms of the low self-image of the black child. If the first response had, in its cruder forms, treated racism as a sickness and located this sickness in the personalities of white, usually working-class, extremists, the second response took a similarly pathological view of racism, locating it this time in the black child's self-concept.

There is a long history to this response, which has come under severe criticism of late. Throughout the 1960s it was a way of explaining failure at school among children of various ethnic and social class groups. According to this explanation working-class children in general and West Indian working-class children in particular are more likely to fail at school because they have a poor self-image, deriving in part at least from their membership of culturally 'deprived' families whose fundamental structures are located in 'deprived' or 'depressed' urban environments. The school's role becomes, therefore, one of compensation for all the supposed inadequacies of the pupil.

From the outset there was resistance among certain groups of inner-city teachers to this notion of compensatory schooling.

It was not until the late 1960s and early 1970s, however, that their counter-arguments were clearly and forcefully articulated by a group of educationists whose work came to be known as the 'new sociology' (see, for example, Young, 1971). The fallacy of the cultural 'deprivation' theory was, they argued, to be found in its focus on the individual child rather than upon the social organization of schooling in which the child is placed.

One of the consequences of this critique was a redefinition of the problem of failure in terms of the school's unwillingness to value anything other than mainstream culture. Such a culture, claimed Nell Keddie, 'is by definition, in the use of indices such as income, occupation, education, etc., a minority culture: the culture of the middle class, which is then said to stand for "society at large" ' (Keddie, 1973, 8). Schools, in other words, require pupils to conform to cultural norms which may be quite alien to them. If teachers want to confront the problem of failure among certain groups of pupils, argued Keddie, they must see it as their own failure to recognize the inherent strength and vitality of the cultures to which these groups belong.

Teachers who took this argument seriously found themselves faced with two immediate tasks. First, there was the need to rethink the content of the school curriculum so that it became more than just a reflection of mainstream culture. Second, there was the equally important need to rethink the relationship between teacher and pupils so that it became more than a one-way channel for transmitting received wisdom. It was in responding to this second need that teachers forged what was to prove a highly significant link between multicultural education and 'progressive' teaching methods. For teachers now had to be in a position to learn from their pupils: their authority lay not so much in what they already knew as in their ability to create structures within which they and their pupils could learn collaboratively.

Ironically, this shift towards a more 'progressive' pedagogy only served to alienate still further the very groups with which the teachers in question were trying to align themselves. In an article in *The Times Educational Supplement* in 1978, Austin and Garrison argued that the West Indian community was responding to educational failure, high unemployment and indifference in both local and central government to the plight of black youths 'by starting its own supplementary schools to provide the skills it considers lacking in formal educational institutions' (Austin and Garrison, 1978). A slightly earlier report in *The Guardian*, claiming that 'old-fashioned learning by rote pays off,' had been the first one to draw attention to the development of these schools by working-class West Indian parents. It provided a serious acknowledgement of the challenge of these schools to the established school system and focused on one of the main grievances of parents who felt it necessary to send their children to supplementary schools: namely, that informal classrooms and 'progressive' teaching methods, which they felt characterized the established school system, were ill-suited to the needs of their children (*Guardian*, 1978).

These views were given intellectual backing by the publication in 1981 of a book by Maureen Stone, entitled *The Education of the Black Child in Britain: the Myth of Multiracial Education*, in which she argues that the theoretical underpinning of multicultural education is at best misconceived and at worst damaging to the life chances of large numbers of children. Drawing on her own research into children's attitudes and aspirations in community-run supplementary schools and in multicultural education projects, she tries to show that the latter undermine the very real aspirations of black children and their parents. Their tacit assumption, she argues, is that black children (a term she uses to denote only children of West Indian origin) will never be socially mobile.

Her own research shows that, in fact, West Indian children do not have a low self-image. They derive the means to sustain a sense of self from many sources and do not rely on negative and hostile views as their source of information about self. Because, according to Stone, multicultural education stresses affective goals of self-expression, self-fulfilment and happiness as the basis of its teaching methods, it distracts teachers from their central concern with teaching or instructing children in the knowledge and skills essential to life in this society. 'Teaching methods associated with the mastery of skills and knowledge and the development of abilities', she argues, 'should be substituted for affective-type goals which are vague, and give teachers access to aspects of pupil personality which should be private' (Stone, 1981, 253).

This brings us to a major weakness in Stone's argument; namely, that it conflates two distinct sets of arguments. One of these centres on the question of educational assumptions and the other on the question of teaching styles. Reacting against both the cultural 'deprivation' theory and informal styles of teaching, she takes for granted that the one necessarily generates the other. Clearly, this may be the case in some instances. However, it is also undoubtedly the case that rationales drawn from the notion of cultural 'deprivation' can generate traditional, instructional styles of teaching; and that informal classrooms can be organized around a principle of deep respect for other cultures. By conflating the arguments Stone is unable to make these kinds of distinctions, which are crucial for teachers attempting to be critical about their own attempts to educate pupils for a multicultural society.

Nevertheless, her first premise, that the 'low self-image' theory is wrong, is important and timely. For the flaw in this theory is to trace the cause of black oppression back to the black community itself. The way in which racism subordinates certain ethnic groups is thereby obscured and important political issues conveniently sidestepped. Any attempt to resolve the pluralist dilemma by means of programmes of work which aim at raising the self-esteem of pupils from minority ethnic groups is, therefore, highly suspect and should be avoided by all those who wish to respond positively to the central theme of Stone's book.

Equally suspect, however, is the jettisoning of all education programmes which employ what Stone calls 'affective-type goals', simply because some of these are based on wrong-headed principles. Take, for example, the following account, by a young girl of Barbadian origin, of a lesson in which the class had been exploring the theme of apartheid:

I think what we found out in the lesson surprised most of the girls. We heard things on television like cricketeers have been blacklisted for playing in South Africa, but we never really understood what it meant and it was really surprising to learn that black people have to live in certain areas; it really did surprise me because we didn't think that anything like that went on anywhere. Julie said she never even heard of the apartheid system. We discovered how people had to live going through that every day of their lives, not being able to go certain places, eat certain things. Sometimes when you thought of it, you just wished it was made up. It was like a shock; you never thought it could be that bad.

It made me feel that a lot more had got to be done. Like we think that our problems are bad, which they are, and then we think of the black people in South Africa and their problems are even worse. Afterwards when we weren't in lessons we got together and talked about it and a lot of us were really shocked as how the people were treated and we said if we could we'd like to do something about it. (Dodgson, 1982, 106–7)

This lesson undoubtedly had 'affective-type goals', if the manner in which it played back upon the pupils' own feelings and emotions is anything to go by. It also, as the full lesson account reveals, took place within an informal classroom environment in which the teacher was at pains to engage the pupils' own powers of self-expression. Yet it in no way assumed a low self-image in the pupils. On the contrary, it assumed their ability to handle challenging material and to adopt a critical and interpretive attitude to the work. To point this out is not to assert the supremacy of one teaching style over another. Rather, it is a matter of contending that the kinds of teaching methods that Maureen Stone would sacrifice have themselves been instrumental in denying the validity of the myth of cultural 'deprivation'. As such they have an important and complementary part to play in the education of pupils for a multicultural society.

A WAY FORWARD

The critics cited in the previous pages – Hazel Carby (1982), Farrukh Dhondy (1982), Chris Mullard (1980) and Maureen Stone (1981) – remind us that genuine equality of opportunity is exceedingly difficult to achieve within the state education system. Carby's accusation that 'multiculturalists had visions of classrooms as microcosms of a race relations paradise' (Carby, 1982, 208) may be sweeping in its generalization, but its import is clear enough: the classroom cannot serve as a refuge from the harsh realities of social inequality. For it is itself implicated in the construction of that inequality. Schools, therefore, can never compensate children for the ills in society. All they can do is confront those ills, both in their own institutional structures and in the content of their curricula. It is this confrontation that constitutes the way forward for multicultural education.

In attempting to extend the pluralist perspective beyond an exclusive concern with diversity, and towards a recognition of the inequality that characterizes that diversity, it is not as yet possible to point to any fully developed set of practices or precepts. What we have to observe is active and pressing, but not yet fully articulated: an emergent, rather than dominant, grouping of ideas and strategies. At best we can locate what may, in retrospect, prove to have been significant growth points in the pedagogy and principles of schooling for a multicultural society.

Institutional racism

The first such growth point is an increasing willingness among teachers to examine their own practice in relation to the notion of racism. This raises the crucial question, which has been implicit in much of the preceding discussion, concerning the adequacy of definitions of racism currently in use. The problem with popular definitions of racism is that they tend to be too restrictive. As we have seen, they ignore the underlying features of racism and concentrate instead on the surface phenomena. What is missing here is any attempt to link conceptually the notion of individual racial prejudice with the structural features of discriminatory policies and practices within the context of British society. The treatment and position of racial minorities within Britain is seen, therefore, in terms of personal feelings alone rather than in terms of the relation between these feelings and the broader social and political issues.

Any adequate definition of racism would have to recognize the ways in which racist arguments set out to justify the unequal treatment of certain groups conceived of as distinct racial categories. What we are beginning to feel our way towards, then, is an approach to racism which cannot be seen simply in terms of personal feelings detached from social structure. A definition is required which embodies a condition whereby those who consider themselves to be superior are instrumental in sustaining a set of relationships based on domination and subordination. The advantage of this approach is that it situates racial practices within a framework of institutional power relationships. The problem of racism is then conceived, not as prejudice, but as domination.

This domination operates, in part at least, at the ideological level. Like all ideologies, racism 'is rarely imposed from above with the conscious aim of deception' (Miles, 1982, 81). It offers us, rather, a set of readily available common-sense explanations of a wide range of issues (rising unemployment, cuts in public expenditure, the reorganization of the forces of law and order, etc.). If racist interpretations are to have credibility then they must, as John Tierney suggests, *'appear* correct according to the individual's own experience of black pupils' (Tierney, 1982, 11). This is precisely how ideologies have force: they present us with beliefs that work.

Given the ideological dimensions of racism, the task for the teacher is to deconstruct the obvious; to challenge the 'taken for granted' assumptions that are the very stuff of institutional racism. While this process of deconstruction involves every aspect of school life, particular attention needs to be given to the question of curriculum content. For it is as part of the curriculum that the issue of racism can become an object of critical analysis. As a minimum requirement the school curriculum should provide every pupil with an understanding of the roots of racism in British colonial history, the manifestations of racism in contemporary British society, and the scientific construction of racism in Western thought. Anything less than a radical reappraisal of the whole curriculum in the light of this requirement reduces multicultural education to mere tokenism.

Minority viewpoints

One way of ensuring that this requirement is met is by building minority perspectives into the content of the curriculum. This is very different from asserting that the curriculum should be relevant *for* pupils from minority groups or that it should be *about* the traditions and customs of such groups (although each of these may well be true). The point being made here is that the curriculum should be reconstructed around the interpretations and perspectives of those who are themselves members of minority groups. It should be developed in partnership *with* them.

A willingness among teachers to learn from black British people about what it means to be black and British constitutes, therefore, a second important growth point in multicultural education. In certain multiracial areas this partnership is beginning to involve active collaboration between schools and minority ethnic groups within the local community. In non-multiracial areas it involves a sensitivity to the viewpoints of the black British community as reflected in whatever published material is available. In both it necessarily leads to an uncovering of those aspects of British society – both its history and its present lived reality – that have hitherto remained hidden and unexamined.

No one is pretending that the incorporation of minority perspectives into the school curriculum is an easy matter. For a start, these perspectives are poorly documented and frequently distorted. The experience of black people in Britain invariably has to pass through the interpretive filter of a white author or presenter before reaching a wider audience (see, for example, Patterson, 1965). Moreover, where the experience is presented by black people themselves (see, for example, Hinds, 1966; Kapo, 1981; and Sivanandan, 1982) it is almost certain to raise social and political issues which, within the context of most schools, will prove to be highly controversial. A commitment to face these issues, coupled with a determination to search out the minority perspective, is a prerequisite of innovative work in the area of multicultural education.

Action and reflection

Both of the growth points mentioned so far have relied upon the willingness of teachers to test their own practice against certain principles. This willingness to see the task of curriculum development as essentially value-laden, and to adopt a correspondingly critical stance to one's own efforts in this area, constitutes the third major growth point in the area of multicultural education. This is the point at which theoretical insight and practical intervention converge.

The emphasis here is not simply on teachers being required to spot aspects of racism in their own teaching. Rather, they are required to see their own teaching as an articulation of their value system. Observing their own 'unintentional racism' may be part of this process. A much more important part, however, is defining through the pedagogical process the positive values implicit in their work. For it is these positive values which present a real alternative to racist assumptions and practices.

One such positive value, on which it is possible to build a broad base of support, is the child's right to know. Any education system could be usefully evaluated by the extent to which it gives its pupils access to socially and personally relevant knowledge. Judged against this criterion multicultural education is concerned less with change than with improvement. For teachers who are aware, for example, of the long and highly significant history of black people in Britain are not only better teachers, but better history teachers; teachers, that is, whose knowledge and expertise reflect with greater accuracy the social reality of British life. Similarly, teachers who know something about, say, the Nigerian novel as developed by Chinua Achebe and Wole Soyinka are thereby better teachers of literature; with a keener sense of the rich potentiality and responsiveness of the novel as an art form.

The premium placed within this argument on the child's right of access to socially relevant knowledge is more than just a matter of raising academic standards. Although limited in its impact and in no way a compensation for material inequality, this increased access represents a move towards a more equal society in which diverse cultures are valued and where minority voices are heard and heeded. The fact that such a society exists as yet only as a utopia means that multicultural education must invariably take the form of critical practice; an ongoing evaluation, by pupils and teacher alike, of their own knowledge and a constant reaching beyond the bounds of their own parochialism. This ought not to blind us to the fact that multicultural education is, however, an articulation in policy and practice of a positive urge towards genuine equality.

In this chapter I have tried to move from an examination of assimilationist assumptions as residual elements within multicultural education, through a critical analysis of its currently dominant pluralist perspective, to a brief review of some alternative and, as yet, only emergent emphases within existing practice. On the basis of this overview, and with particular reference to the growth points described in the latter part of this chapter, the purpose of multicultural education might be described in terms of the following general curricular aims:

1 To raise the pupils' awareness of racism as a key element in the power relation between cultures and as a major influence upon their own and other people's lives.

2 To increase their knowledge and understanding of the history, cultural heritage, and values of minority ethnic groups within the local community and within the wider context of British society.
3 To enable pupils to adopt a global perspective on issues of contemporary concern and to gain an understanding of multicultural Britain in its world context.

The following chapter outlines the broad structures of curriculum change within which these aims can begin to be translated into an effective whole-school strategy.

CHAPTER THREE

Policy into Practice

How can a serious consideration of institutional racism work its way onto the school curriculum? How can the school begin to enable pupils to recognize and combat such racism? How can the individual teacher, operating within an institution that is itself a transmitter of racist values, act as more than an agent of socialization? How can she educate for a multicultural society in the sense of enabling pupils to value minority viewpoints and become aware of the extent to which their own views are shaped by cultural factors? This chapter sets out to address these questions.

Two broad organizational structures within which the curriculum can be developed to meet the needs of a multicultural society are outlined in the following pages: 'accretion' and 'permeation'. Throughout, the stress is upon the need to create a close fit between policy and practice; between statements of intent, with which we have so far been mainly concerned, and what actually happens in the classroom. No blueprint for the instant implementation of policy statements or the immediate achievement of prespecified goals is offered. The best that can be hoped for is that, through a sensitive appraisal of the issues involved and of the conditions pertaining in particular schools, teachers might gradually create a context of ideas and action in which individual initiatives begin to have an impact in unexpected quarters.

THE LIMITS OF ACCRETION

'Accretion' is a term used to denote the notion of multicultural education as a process of adding extraneous matter to an existing curriculum structure, rather than as a process of restructuring the whole curriculum in the light of new insights and materials. Broadly, three kinds of curriculum structures, which adhere to the organizational principle of accretion and are currently operating in schools, can be distinguished:

Multicultural education as an optional extra. The multicultural education programme operating in many schools is offered as part of a formal or informal option pool. A school, for example, may well feel that its concern for multicultural education is adequately met by the provision of a CSE course in World Studies. Similarly, a Black Studies Club, say, or tuition for a steel-drum ensemble, may be offered as part of the programme of extra-curricular activities of the school. The advantage of such a system is obvious; it gives an opportunity to motivated pupils to explore in depth the implications of their own membership of a multicultural society. The disadvantages, however, are equally obvious. For multicultural education when offered as an optional extra caters only for a small number of pupils. Those whose need for such a course is greatest may be the least likely to opt for it.

Multicultural education as a common core. The multicultural education programme of a school may also take the form of a discrete and compulsory course for all pupils. Such a course operates as part of a core curriculum and may well be integrated with work in, say, Health Education or Moral Education. Unlike the previous structure, this has the advantage of being a compulsory component and therefore of value to all pupils regardless of personal motivation. Its major disadvantage lies in the fact that it fails to relate the issues with which it deals to the curriculum as a whole. Where multicultural education is restricted to a common core course the pupil may well not see its relevance to the whole range of subjects represented on the curriculum. The impact of such a course is thereby severely limited. Understanding of racism does not constitute a distinct category of human learning, but a dimension of our existing categories. Indeed, the boundaries of these categories may well set a limit to our recognition and understanding of racism as an issue.

Multicultural education as piecemeal development. A more sophisticated approach to multicultural education presents the issue of racism as a component on a variety of different courses. The Biology Department, the English Department, the History Department, each adds a couple of units to its existing course in order to raise the relevant issues. Other departments follow suit. Soon multicultural education is represented as a component on most of the courses operating within the school. The problem with such an approach is that it makes no attempt to rethink the subject syllabus in terms of the new material. Although multicultural education is now diffused across the curriculum, the content of individual syllabuses may remain hopelessly ethnocentric (with the exception of those few, isolated units which constitute the school's token gesture on behalf of anti-racist practice).

The chief objection to these three ways of embedding multicultural education in the school curriculum is that they enable, even encourage, both pupils and teachers to minimize, compartmentalize or sidestep issues relating to racism. This happens because the curriculum as perceived by those who actually plan it may be very different from the curriculum as experienced by the pupil. Curriculum planners have a tendency to see the 'whole' curriculum synchronically; as a diagram of who is teaching what to whom and where at any one time. For the child, however, the 'whole' curriculum is experienced diachronically; as a long plod from subject to subject, classroom to classroom, and teacher to teacher. Features which are prominent on the large-scale map which constitutes the curriculum planner's frame of reference may, therefore, be barely discernible on the pathway taken by the individual child. The limits of accretion are marked by the intersection of these two, often opposing, perspectives.

Nevertheless, within its own, albeit limited, terms of reference what I have here referred to as accretion can enable at least some pupils to think through the question of racism. To those teachers who have developed, or are in the process of developing, such a curriculum, it may seem unfair to label their efforts as tokenism. At least they are doing something. Moreover, it should be acknowledged that accretion may be a necessary stage, within many institutions, on the road towards a more fully developed policy on multicultural education. For by raising within their own subject area questions of general curricular concern a small group of committed teachers may be using the most effective means available of alerting the staff as a whole to a new set of educational issues. As an end in itself, however, accretion is not enough. What is needed is a way of embedding multicultural education in the school curriculum in such a way that the issues it raises are fully related to what every child learns in each subject area.

THE PERMEATION PROCESS

An alternative to accretion can be found in a strategy that is often referred to as 'permeation'. Here curriculum development in the field of multicultural education is seen, not in terms of additions to an existing structure, but in terms of rethinking and restructuring every aspect of the curriculum. Issues relating to multicultural education, in other words, are allowed to soak into the very fibre of schooling. Since the development of this strategy is one of the most significant initiatives to have been undertaken in this field over the last ten years, I shall discuss it in some detail. However, it is important to realize that the process of permeation cannot be completed overnight. It is part of a long and often disturbing progression, involving critical review and cautious innovation. I shall, therefore, describe this strategy in terms of three necessary and overlapping phases of development.

Phase 1: Small-scale innovation

To be effective any school policy on multicultural education must be grounded in the insights which have emerged from practical initiatives taken in the classroom. Such initiatives, as varied as the contexts within which they take place, are likely nevertheless to share some common characteristics. First, they are usually small-scale, not in the sense of being of little educational value, but in the sense of their being operative within a circumscribed area of school life. For this very reason, of course, they may be overlooked by those members of staff who are not involved in, or immediately affected by, the innovation. One of the prime functions of a headteacher in such a situation is to ensure that isolated initiatives are discussed and understood by the staff as a whole.

Secondly, such initiatives are often subject-based. Not surprisingly, perhaps, teachers committed to raising their own awareness of issues invariably begin from within the framework of their own subject specialism. Their own training and, within the secondary sector at least, the organizational and curricular structure of the institutions within which they work reinforce this tendency. In itself it is no bad thing. A teacher's expertise within her own subject area may sharpen perceptions, inform insights, and suggest practical ways of implementing new ideas. The drawback, however, is that the subject-boundedness of the innovation may detract from its impact across the curriculum.

This limitation is partially offset by the third characteristic of the small-scale innovations we are here discussing – namely, the fact that they are team-based. The individual teacher working in complete isolation at the task of curriculum development is likely to face apthy, incomprehension, and even open hostility from some members of staff. The likelihood is that unless such a teacher is able to create links with other teachers committed to similar concerns and issues she is likely to become cynical about the possibility of ever bringing about any appreciable change within the institution as a whole. Effective small-scale innovations, therefore, are invariably carried through by a committed team of teachers who can draw upon one another's strengths and sustain one another's morale.

There is a further reason why effective innovation in the field of multicultural education tends to be team-based. Invariably the education that teachers have themselves received is ethnocentric and therefore a poor preparation for developing an anti-racist curriculum. By working together teachers can pool their knowledge and their skills, share materials and resources, and divide the labour of researching hidden areas of their own specialisms. The team, in other words, not only lends moral support to the individuals involved, but also informs and structures their joint endeavour. It constitutes the innovative thrust of their work.

Let me give an example. At Vauxhall Manor School in south London three teachers have recently been working on a third-year history course with the help of the warden of the local History and Social Sciences Teachers' Centre. The following brief extract is taken from their account of this work in progress:

Is the appropriate response from history teachers to the challenge of multicultural education to focus on world history? To some extent yes – but we believe it is equally important for pupils to study the history of the society in which they live in order to gain greater understanding of their place in it. Approached in a way that reflects the historic cultural diversity of our society, the study of British history can be part of an anti-racist curriculum.

At Vauxhall Manor School, an inner city girls' comprehensive in south London which draws pupils from diverse cultural backgrounds, we have put this idea into practice in the third year. We take migration as our central theme, concentrating on the basic concepts underlying the movement of people and the development of multicultural societies. We consider this course to be equally relevant in multicultural schools and those with a seemingly 'indigenous' intake.

The backbone of this one year course is a series of case studies, illustrating the reasons for migration at particular times, comparing the experiences of migrants themselves and assessing the contribution of various groups in British society. Since method is as important as content we have devised materials around historical concepts and skills which encourage pupils to analyse events for themselves.

Our material – designed for mixed ability classes – consists of a series of booklets which provide a structure; they do not represent worksheet teaching and pupils are directed to a range of written and visual resources. (*Times Educational Supplement*, 1982, 27)

Clearly, we have here an example of a small-scale innovation that is both subject-centred and team-based. It is interesting to note, however, that the four teachers involved in this initiative represent a range of subject specialisms: drama, history, and the social sciences. The expertise they are able to draw on – in terms of both teaching methods and curriculum content – is, therefore, considerable. It is precisely this range of skilled reference which allows them to develop the variety of new materials that are needed for such a course. Without a willingness on their behalf to move beyond their own individual know-how and learn from one another the initiative would be doomed.

A further point needs stressing. This course illustrates the importance of both teachers *and* pupils adopting a research stance to their work. It relies upon the discovery of new facts and new perspectives. It does not depend solely upon the personal experiences of those within the teaching group. For that very reason it is a course which, as Carol Adams points out in the extract quoted above, is 'equally relevant in multicultural schools and those with a seemingly "indigenous" intake'. This is not to say that the course fails to engage the feelings and emotions of the class, but that these feelings and emotions are not in themselves the objects of enquiry. Multicultural education, in this context, is much more than a therapeutic diversion; it is a serious attempt, on behalf of those with responsibility for curriculum planning, to respond to the need for an informed understanding of cultural diversity. What is being developed in this third-year history course is a knowledge-based curriculum.

Phase 2: Coordination and development

There comes a point, of course, when the kind of small-scale innovations exemplified by the third-year history course at Vauxhall Manor needs to be coordinated within the broad curriculum framework of the school. Timing here is crucial. It is essential that the school as a whole commits itself to building on its existing strengths, rather than merely formulating an abstract statement of intent which may be far removed from the everyday reality of the classroom. Experimental and developmental work by groups of teachers must, therefore, precede the drafting of a policy statement, if such a policy is ever to have any validity.

The dangers of relying exclusively on the formulation of policy statements was highlighted recently by a survey into the relation between policy and practice in multicultural education. This survey was conducted by Barry Troyna and Wendy Ball, of the SSRC Research Unit on Ethnic Relations at the University of Aston, and was carried out among headteachers in a north of England education authority which had, two years previously, produced a policy on this theme. Seventy-one headteachers were interviewed on a range of issues relating to multicultural education. Perhaps the best guide to the institutional response of their schools to the authority's directives was provided by the headteachers' response to the question: 'Would you say your school was involved in multicultural education?' Considering the priority attached to this issue by the local education authority and the relatively large amount of its scarce resources deployed in its development, it is, as Troyna and Ball pointed out, 'alarming that twenty-four heads freely admitted that their schools were not involved. Put bluntly, over a third of our sample had blatantly ignored the authority's policy prescription' (Troyna and Ball, 1983).

It would be a pity, however, if as a result of these findings policy development were written off as a purely academic exercise. The findings should remind us of the need for practice and policy to go hand in hand. The formulation of a curriculum policy on multicultural education by every school and every local education authority remains an urgent professional obligation. A rationale for the drawing up of such policies was established as early as September 1982 by one of several working parties convened by the Afro-Caribbean Education Resource Project to follow up issues raised in the Rampton Report (Department of Education and Science, 1981):

We submit that all schools throughout the country should draw up a School Policy on Multiethnic Education as a matter of urgency:

(1) To promote the principles embodied in the U.N. Charter of Human Rights and E.E.C. directives.
(2) To prepare all pupils for life in a pluralist society in which there is social and racial harmony.
(3) To counter the damaging effects of ethnocentricity.
(4) To counter the presence of overt racism in the schools where ethnic minorities are present and throughout the country.
(5) To counter the factors contributing to underachievement of West Indian and other groups as identified in the report.
(6) To create an educational and social climate which promotes strong motivation and a positive approach to educational achievement amongst all ethnic groups.
(7) To prevent negative, patronising or stereotyped views amongst teachers and pupils in schools and in society as a whole.
(8) To instil in all young people confidence and pride in their own cultural roots and linguistic repertoire.
(9) To extend social relationships across ethnic groups and develop an appreciation of other cultures.

(10) To show pupils that the school values them as individuals as well as members of ethnic and cultural groups.
(11) To provide equality of opportunity.
(12) To act as a positive agent for social change. (Afro-Caribbean Education Resource Project, 1982, 1)

Clearly, as far as the Afro-Caribbean Education Resource Project was – and is – concerned, there are some very good reasons why schools and local education authorities should formulate a policy on multicultural education, both as a means of affirming commitment to anti-racist practice and of communicating this commitment to both pupils and parents. The question, then, is: How can such a policy be developed and what elements should it contain?

In order to answer that question we need to remind ourselves that no two schools are alike. The curriculum policy developed by any school will depend upon a number of factors, some of which are unique to that particular setting. The intake of the school, for example, its size, and the available resources on which it can draw, are all variables that influence the scope of curriculum planning within the institution. Success within the curriculum planning process can be judged to a very large extent by the sensitivity of the teachers involved to the constraints and possibilities inherent in the specific situation within which they work.

Many of the factors influencing the development of school policy in the area of multicultural education are, however, common to all schools. The most important to these has to do with the general ethos of the school; its capacity for encouraging and supporting a collaborative approach to curriculum planning. Clearly, this is a difficult quality to define. However, it fronts onto some crucial issues: the willingness of the headteacher to delegate responsibility, for example, and the existence of a democratic decision-making process within the school. Without these, any staff working party which sets out to develop a whole-school curriculum policy on multicultural education is likely to find itself both marginalized and powerless.

In setting up such a working party attention needs to be paid, therefore, to its membership. It is essential, for a start, that the full range of subject areas should be represented. For only then can multicultural education be seen as a cross-curricular issue and the debate about multicultural education begin to be conducted across the spread of subjects. It is also important that the membership of such a working party should be drawn from the various ranks of the management structure. The concerns of a head of department, say, may be very different from those of a probationary teacher, while those of a head of year or head of house will be different again. Each set of concerns needs to be reflected in the membership of the working party and equal weight given to each contribution regardless of the status of the particular teacher concerned.

Attention also needs to be paid to the way in which the working party is to keep the staff as a whole informed about its progress and remain open to the views and opinions of as many people as possible. Clearly, regular progress reports at staff meetings are important in this respect, but other kinds of reportage might also be used. For example, a monthly bulletin might be circulated in order to keep colleagues up to date on recent developments and to request any necessary information. The working party should aim to be as open as possible, while at the same time keeping its membership to a manageable size.

The dangers of allowing the working party to become isolated from the mainstream of the school have been usefully documented in the report produced by the Birley High School group in Manchester and referred to in the previous chapter:

> Above all it rapidly became clear that we had not adequately explained our aims to the staff as a whole. Partly because of prejudice and emotion and partly because it coincided with the arrival of a new headmaster, the working party faced formidable antagonism and suspicion. The atmosphere of cynicism towards the work was substantial and became overt in several meetings. There were times when it seemed that suicide . . . was the only option for the working party. (Birley High School, 1980, 3)

In spite of this death-wish, the working party survived; but only by opening its doors to new members of staff, creating links with neighbouring schools, and inviting along represent-atives from local ethnic minority communities. The discussions resulting from these meetings revealed to the members of the working party the extent to which they had hitherto been seen as operating in 'a closed community' (ibid., 4).

A prime task facing the members of any working party on multicultural education is finding a way of being able to talk together. The issues are in some instances so threatening and the vested interests so varied that initially discussion may be difficult. To begin with the talk is likely to be circuitous and anecdotal. Although it is useful to draw up a schedule early on so as to give a sense of purpose to the venture, detailed plans of action should be avoided until differences have been fully discussed. Differences of opinion, it should be noted, do not always have to be resolved. They do, however, have to be clearly articulated and mutually understood if there is to be any possibility of team effort. It should always be remembered that the effective formulation and implementation of a policy will depend to a large extent on the sensitivity of the group to the issues under discussion. No amount of activity can compensate for a basic lack of understanding concerning what these issues are and how, within the school and wider community, opinions on these issues may be deeply divided.

Bearing this in mind some useful starting points during the early meetings of the group might be: (1) looking at the pattern of cultural diversity within the local community; (2) understanding what racism is, its historical context, and how it manifests itself in contemporary society; (3) considering how racism can and does operate within the existing school curriculum; (4) reviewing the materials and resources that inform work in the classroom.

Having discussed these points in some detail, and kept the staff as a whole informed about the deliberations, the working party will need to set about the task of monitoring the staff's views on specific issues and noting examples of good practice. This may be done by questionnaire, interview, or small-group meetings. The latter is probably the most common, althought a combination of the three methods may well prove more effective. The working party should bear in mind that some of the teachers whose views and practices are being monitored are likely to feel extremely threatened. Clearly, every effort should be made by members of the working party to avoid the impression that they are involving colleagues in a crude accountability exercise. The real point of the exercise is coordination and development: the linking of isolated initiatives into a purposeful consideration by the whole school of issues relating to multicultural education.

In placing these issues firmly on the school agenda and

making time for their discussion and development, the working party would need to view the curriculum task in its broadest possible setting. Questions concerning the content and organization of the curriculum would have to be seen in relation to the question of teaching styles and methods, of attitudes and expectations held by the teacher, and of pupil selection and grouping. This assumption of a broad curriculum perspective is made explicit by the staff of Quintin Kynaston School in the policy statement in their staff handbook (1980). For here a section on 'knowledge about race, culture and racism', as it relates to the overt curriculum, is inserted between sections which highlight issues in the hidden curriculum, as these relate to 'comprehensive school aims' and the need for 'being vigilant' with regard to racist behaviour among pupils.

The assumption of a broad curriculum perspective is also explicit in the curriculum statement included in the North Westminster Community School document, entitled *Towards a Multicultural Philosophy*:

> The curriculum, explicit and hidden, must aim, through the over-arching whole-school policies, the separate subject department syllabuses, the tutorial programme, and all curriculum planning:
>
> i) to create an understanding of an interest in different environments, societies, systems and cultures across the world.
>
> ii) to study the political, social and economic reasons for racism and inequality, and their present-day effects in this country and the world.
>
> iii) to encourage pupils to recognise that each society has its own values, traditions and everyday living patterns which should be considered in the context of that society.
>
> iv) to study scientific achievements outside the western world, and alternative approaches to science.
>
> v) to explore and share the ideas, opinions and interests which derive from particular cultural experiences. Its content should be so selected that it engages pupils' feelings as well as giving them skills and information.
>
> vi) to develop the concepts and skills which will allow pupils to criticise and actively participate in all social institutions, e.g., media, political parties, etc. (North Westminster Community School, 1982)

Whatever form the final policy document takes it should include some reference to the four cornerstones of curriculum planning:

- *Content*, which should reflect the multicultural, multiracial nature of British society, past and present.
- *Styles of teaching*, which should be sensitive to the need for both pupils and teachers to enquire beyond their own received assumptions.
- *Teacher expectations*, which should be equally high (in respect of intellectual achievement and social behaviour) for all pupils regardless of cultural background.
- *Selection and grouping*, which should be free of any bias resulting from the conscious or unconscious stereotyping of particular cultural groups.

This is by no means an exhaustive list of essential elements, but it does provide a firm foundation for further developments, some of which will be outlined in more detail in the following chapters. It is worth repeating, moreover, that in regarding the above as necessary topics to be included in any curriculum policy, we are purposely stretching the term 'curriculum' to cover the hidden as well as the overt structures of learning within the school. This is an essential procedure if the development by schools of curriculum policies on multicultural education is to be anything other than a cosmetic exercise.

Phase 3: Consultation and evaluation

The drafting of a policy statement is only one phase – albeit a central phase – of the permeation process. Unless the initial drafting is followed by a period of consultation both within the school itself and in the wider educational and community context, then the policy is unlikely to have much impact. Within the school, as we have seen, the policy needs to be discussed across the full range of forums: staff meetings, departmental meetings, meetings of the pastoral staff, etc. It is also important that the secretarial and caretaking staff of the school are involved in these discussions. Theirs is a significant contribution to the ethos of the school and their insights and understandings ought, therefore, to inform the debate at every level.

Outside the school three groups in particular need to be considered in relation to the task of consultation. The first of these is, of course, the parents. As a bare minimum all parents need informing of the policy, its implications, and of their rights and responsibilities with regard to the issues it discusses. Schools serving a multiracial catchment area will need to ensure that the policy is translated into the various languages used within the locality. There also, however, ought to be opportunities for interested parents to talk to staff about the policy, to offer their own viewpoint, and to suggest, if necessary, radical changes to the document.

It is, though, only through its implementation that the implications of the policy will be fully understood by the parents. Needless to say this understanding will not necessarily lead to universal approbation. In attempting to consult with parents the school will necessarily encounter implicitly racist views. It will also, however, gain the respect of significant sections within the parental group. Ways should be found of locating and mobilizing these sections so that they can be used as an informing and educative unit within the whole community of the school. The dialogue between parents and school is an essential element in the effective implementation of any curriculum policy on multicultural education.

The creation of such a dialogue, however, is dependent upon the school first creating an atmosphere that is open and welcoming in its routine transactions with parents. Brent Teachers' Association, in their discussion document *Multicultural Education in Brent Schools*, spelt out this need for a school environment that facilitates discussion and contact between parents and teachers:

> Teachers must be aware of varying parental attitudes to school and their concept of school. Schools are thought to have very different functions by different cultural groups. Schools must be aware of this and ensure that parents feel they are welcome in school and are participants in the educational process. This kind of contact can be established by involving the parents in, for example, the school's social functions to familiarise them with the idea that the school is not an alien body which excludes them from the children's development. It is also necessary to communicate adequately; to send information to parents in a language that they find intelligible (the actual

language used and the manner of its use); and for teachers to be prepared to visit homes. (Brent Teachers' Association, 1980, 8–9)

Without an already well-established dialogue between parents and teachers on a range of educational issues and in a variety of social settings, it would clearly be very difficult for any school to initiate effective consultation procedures with parents on a proposed policy for multicultural education. The latter should be seen as a natural extension of the ongoing debate between school and local community and not as an isolated initiative that bears no relation to the life and work of the school as a whole.

A second group which needs to be consulted with regard to any proposed policy on multicultural education comprises potential employers of school leavers. The Race Relations Act of 1976 (Part II, Section 14 (1), (2) and (3)) places the onus upon employment agencies and local education authorities to ensure that school leavers seeking employment are not discriminated against on racial grounds. Those involved in the recruiting and employment of school leavers should be invited to contribute to the debate within schools on multicultural education, with a long-term view to exploring its implications for the world of work and, if necessary, extending its terms of reference to their own circumstances.

Employers are more likely to be drawn into this debate if links have already been created between themselves and the school. Many schools have pioneered projects similar to the School to Work Project at Vauxhall Manor. This particular project includes a sixth-form course for pupils who are not being entered for either Ordinary or Advanced level GCE examinations and a work-experience scheme offered to all fourth- and fifth-year pupils. Issues relating to multicultural education and equal opportunities are likely to arise quite naturally in the course of both these ventures, which can be seen, therefore, as useful means of opening up a debate on these matters between teachers, pupils and employers.

The local education service constitutes a third group which the school needs to consult in shaping its policy on multicultural education. Three agencies in particular require careful consideration. The advisory staff, whose brief is often limited to specific subject areas, may be of use in suggesting practical curriculum strategies. Teachers' centres may also offer facilities and materials designed to be of help to the classroom teacher. Since its responsibility is towards a community of schools, a centre can obviously offer a much broader range of resources than can a single school.

As part of the local education service, institutions of higher education may also in certain crucial respects be able to cater for the needs of the classroom teacher. Those involved in the initial and inservice education of teachers, and in educational research, are becoming increasingly concerned that their work should incorporate the teacherly perspective. Links with higher education may, therefore, provide the teacher with, say, the occasional services of someone who is a skilled classroom observer and who could act as consultant or informal evaluator within the classroom context (see, for example, Nixon and Verrier, 1979). In this situation, of course, the teacher would retain overall control of what was taught and how; the job of the observer would be to pinpoint some of the problems and implications of the teacher's choice of strategies.

The consultation procedures, which we have here briefly reviewed in terms of a number of agencies, ought not to be seen as mere academic exercises. If taken seriously, they should lead to significant improvements and extensions to the school policy on multicultural education. They should also impress upon all those whose interests front onto the life of the school that the staff as a whole means business with regard to the education of all pupils for life in a multicultural society. Above all, however, the insights derived from these consultation procedures should lead to an increase in the quality and quantity of small-scale innovations initiated by teachers within their own classrooms.

Permeation as outlined in this section thus becomes a cyclical process. Small-scale innovations create the need for a coordinated policy, the development of which requires consultation with a wide range of agencies and interested parties. This round of consultation and informal evaluation in turn creates the impetus for renewed innovations at the classroom level, thereby triggering the process once more (see figure 2.) Conceived in these terms permeation as a whole-school strategy takes a great deal of time and patience to develop. For it relies upon the willingness of teachers to modify, not only their practice, but also their attitudes and assumptions. The task of changing perceptions is central to the permeation process.

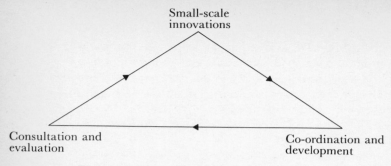

Figure 2 *The cyclical process of permeation*

CHANGING PERCEPTIONS

It would be misleading to suggest that enthusiastic and pioneering teachers by their open approach and effective communications can alone leven the lump of the school. A number of factors conspire against such easy optimism; not least of which is the fact that the working party may be perceived as trouble-makers or, even more damning, as makers of extra work. How, then, are the fundamentalists in the biology department, for example, or the conservatives in the history department, to be persuaded of the pervasive influence and presence of institutional racism? This is a serious question and one where practical suggestions are urgently needed. To ignore it is to ignore the political and sociological reality of the average staff and the power relations within the system.

One way of tackling this question is to focus on the queries that colleagues actually raise rather than on the more esoteric problems that are often imported into the staffroom by well-meaning working parties. Below are some typical questions, statements and issues that are used repeatedly by teachers to justify their own inaction with regard to multicultural education. There is perhaps not a school in Britain where, with a little probing, one would fail to unearth each of the following stock responses. Indeed, it was in often heated discussion over such responses that the argument of the previous three chapters was gradually refined and developed. The following pointers represent, therefore, a summary of some of the major themes of the last three chapters.

Why do we need multicultural education when we have hardly any black pupils?

Multicultural education is, primarily, sound education all round for all pupils. It helps them to understand the place that they, their country and their society have in the world and to think in terms that are internationalist. It shows the positive contribution that minority groups have made and can make in every field of life and reveals the inequalities within contemporary society.

I never think of the colour of a person's skin: I see everyone as being equal.

A desire to affirm the dignity of each individual ought not to blind us to the fact that individuals are members of groups and that some of these groups are, within our society, severely disadvantaged. Between 1973 and 1982, to give but a single example, the increase in registered unemployment among black people was 206% higher than the corresponding increase among white people (Race and Immigration, 1983, 7). To ignore the colour of a person's skin may be a way of turning a blind eye to the continuing influence of racial discrimination.

By talking about racism you'll only succeed in stirring up more trouble.

It is much better that pupils should talk about it in the context of an informed discussion than that they should receive misleading impressions from biased sources to which they will be, and probably already are, exposed in their daily lives. It is our duty as teachers to inform correctly and not to avoid important issues. Pupils have a right to know about racism as it manifests itself both in contemporary society and in history.

White people don't have a monopoly on racism.

The racial prejudice of the white person has a very different significance in our society from the racial prejudice of black people. The former is directed at minority groups and is specifically endorsed and sustained by the power of the state and its dominant cultural structures. While racial prejudice of any kind is reprehensible, the prejudice of the black child cannot be compared, in terms of its social and political significance, with that of the white child.

I don't have enough time to cover the syllabus in its present form and you're urging me to add even more material.

Not necessarily. It might be that you simply need to select different examples or highlight other sets of issues; to adopt a different perspective on what you already teach rather than set about teaching something else. If, however, that is not the case and you are unable to work within the constraints of the existing syllabus, bear in mind that it is not carved on tablets of stone. Even within the public examination system you are at liberty to shop around for an alternative which would be better suited to your needs and interests.

Why don't they integrate?

Given the social inequality of British society, integration would necessarily involve an acceptance by the members of minority ethnic groups of themselves as second-class citizens. If British culture is ever to be genuinely 'civilized', it will have to resist the urge towards cultural domination which is masked by that term 'integration'. Presumably this is what Mahatma Ghandi was getting at when, in reply to someone who asked him what he thought of English civilization, he said, 'I think it would be a good idea.'

To sum up. This chapter has spelled out some of the limitations of simply adding separate units onto an existing structure by way of developing a curricular response to the needs of a multicultural society. I have argued, instead, that a policy of permeation, whereby responsibility for curriculum review and development rests with the whole staff, best answers these needs. Such a policy, however, can only be developed gradually. Three overlapping phases have been suggested as necessary to this process of permeation: (1) small-scale innovation; (2) coordination and development; (3) consultation and evaluation. Finally, the central importance of the teachers' own perceptions has been stressed and the need – in any attempt at curriculum change – to begin with the teachers' own assumptions and attitudes. Our capacity to restructure the curriculum depends, in other words, upon our willingness to work together as teachers on restructuring our own thinking about what constitutes socially relevant knowledge and appropriate practice in, and for, a multicultural society. The mesh of social relationships within which this professional reorientation must be achieved is the subject of the following chapter.

CHAPTER FOUR

Relationships within the School

Multicultural education is grounded in the social relationships of the school: relationships, that is, between teachers, between pupils and teachers, and between the pupils themselves. It is the quality of these relationships – their capacity for equal partnership and sensitivity to the others' needs – that determines to a very large extent the quality of the education programme being offered. This chapter, then, looks at the school as a social environment and discusses its potential as a means of supporting and enriching initiatives within the field of multicultural education.

PROFESSIONAL COLLABORATION

Mutually supportive relationships between teachers are crucial in this respect. The importance of teachers collaborating on the planning and implementation of curricula has already been stressed. However, it may be useful at this point to distinguish some of the forms that this collaboration can take and to spell out the institutional conditions it relies on. Teachers not only need to find their own ways of working together. They also need to be clear about the demands that these ways of working will make on the institution as a whole.

All too often it is assumed that 'professional collaboration' simply means 'team-teaching'. Of course, it may do; but not necessarily. Collaborative work between teachers should also take the form of planning together and gaining feedback from one another. Indeed, without these other two elements any team-teaching is likely to be extremely limited in its impact. Teachers can collaborate while not actually teaching together in the same classroom. They cannot be said to be collaborating, however, unless there is some attempt at joint deliberation and evaluation. Serious discussion of the 'what', 'why' and 'how' of teaching is a prerequisite of effective professional collaboration.

This process of talking through the practice and principles of one's own teaching makes particular demands upon the teachers involved. No team is created overnight. Learning to work together takes time and a great deal of effort and patience. Initially, it may even be a threatening or disturbing experience. It certainly was for the two Birmingham teachers who talked about their attempt to develop a course of lessons in which fourth- and fifth-year secondary pupils used improvised drama as a means of exploring instances of racism in contemporary society:

Interviewer: Is it interesting working together?

Gwen: Well, no, it has driven us potty, let's be honest. Because we feel we don't know each other as human beings any more. We don't talk to each other socially any more. We don't get enough time. I don't ask Linda how she is or what colour she is going to paint her ceiling.

Linda: You see, we have done quite a lot of work in halfterm and in the evenings trying to plan lessons. Gwen has only just has this lesson freed now. Normally, she has had to go off and teach . . .

Gwen: Straight away, as soon as that is over.

Linda: . . . which is very difficult. But now it has been arranged, because we have had a lot of problems with this work; a lot has been done to get her free as we have had to get together to talk after the lessons at night and at halfterm. You see, we don't talk to each other any more about family and children and homes and the pleasantries . . .

Gwen: We look at each other and think 'ah! ah!' . . . I kept asking Linda 'Am I going to have a nervous breakdown?'

Linda:	I think that if we could have had a whole term with no other commitments, no other pressures, it could have been fabulous.
Gwen:	And we would have worked out a really good programme ...
Linda:	We have made a hell of a lot of mistakes.

The mistakes were perhaps inevitable. After all, innovatory work necessarily involves exploring some tracks which turn out to be dead-ends. Nevertheless, listening to these teachers talk about their experience of team-based curriculum development one is left with the impression that if the school as a whole had been more responsive to their needs, some of the strain might have been avoided. Work of this kind, in other words, makes heavy demands on the institution as well as upon the individual. A failure to meet these institutional demands may put an intolerable strain on the innovator.

Clearly, there are limits to the flexibility of any system. However, it should be recognized by heads, deputy heads, and all those with managerial responsibility within the school, that curriculum development in the area of multicultural education is costly. That cost, moreover, should not have to be met solely in terms of the nervous energy of committed teachers. The implications of innovation should be thoroughly discussed and suitable timetabling and staffing arrangements be made. For the social relationships which inform and support effective team work are determined to a large extent by factors outside the control of the teachers themselves. Inflexible timetabling, overcrowded classrooms and insufficient time for preparation and evaluation create a social context in which professional collaboration is virtually impossible.

Such factors are of little consequence, however, unless teachers themselves are willing to learn from one another and so push forward the boundaries of their own practice. Collaborative learning of this kind, as we have seen, is never easy, but it can be made easier if the following points are borne in mind:

- Always be ready to listen to other people's ideas.
- Be willing, when necessary, to adapt or even abandon your own ideas in order to develop someone else's.
- Be willing to discuss underlying principles as well as teaching methods and curriculum content.

- Try not to take criticism personally – relate to it in terms of the issues it raises rather than the defensive feelings it may arouse.
- Outline some sort of schedule. (You will probably not keep to this, but it will nevertheless provide a useful means of plotting the progress of the group.)
- Prepare for all meetings, however informal, that you have together – come with your ideas worked out and make sure you have completed whatever task you may have taken on.

The onus is on each individual to use the time put aside for discussion to the best possible advantage: hence, the need for preparation by all the teachers involved for all meetings. It is also important to ensure that the hierarchical structure of schooling does not serve to block the responses of younger, less experienced colleagues. If the notion of collaboration is to have any meaning, those with senior responsibility within the school must be able to talk as equals to those who have no such responsibility. This is not to say that the equality will necessarily spill over into every sphere of the professional relationships in question: the head of department, for example, will still have overall responsibility for the running of the department and the head of year for the organization of tutorial guidance. It does mean, however, that each idea will be valued on merit, rather than because of the status of the person putting it forward.

Obvious though these points may be they are often overlooked. Collaboration is a difficult experience for many teachers, particularly in its early stages. Since the object of the exercise is, in part at least, to examine one's own assumptions in the light of new insights and ideas, some intellectual reorientation is inevitable. Such reorientation is not without its disorientating side-effects. These, however, can be kept to a minimum if teachers approach the task with a genuine desire to listen to, and learn from, one another. What is needed is an atmosphere which affords sufficient security for teachers to be able to discuss their mistakes and worries frankly and openly.

In a supportive atmosphere of this kind the rewards of professional collaboration far outweigh any difficulties that teachers may experience in learning to work together. There are, for a start, always other people to bounce ideas off; people with different strengths, whose talents may complement and extend one's own. Nor are teachers the only ones to benefit from this flow of ideas. The sense of excitement and commitment which it generates rubs off on the pupils as well. Moreover, the kind of pupils tasks and activities which are devised within a collaborative framework are likely to be more varied given the different subject specialisms and interests which the different members of the teaching team bring to bear on the project.

PUPILS AND TEACHERS

The quality of the relationships between pupils and teachers, and between the pupils themselves, is a further factor determining, within the social environment of the school, the impact of the teachers' attempts to educate for a multicultural society. Pupils have a vital part to play in the process of collaboration. Indeed, if this process is not extended to include the pupils themselves, then whatever innovations are attempted in the name of multicultural education are likely to be severely limited. Anyone concerned with establishing within a school the conditions necessary for change should pay particular attention to the ways in which pupils and teachers can begin to learn together.

One way is for teachers always to make explicit to pupils the point and purpose of any task that is set. Pupils' own perceptions of innovation are rarely monitored, or even acknowledged, when developmental work is attempted in schools. Yet, these perceptions effect quite profoundly the value of the work undertaken. No matter how clearly thought out a scheme of work may be, it will fail if the pupils have no frame of reference by which to grasp its significance. The first task of the innovator is, therefore, to explain to the class why they are doing what they are doing and to discuss with them their own feelings about the task.

Without this degree of openness it is impossible to create an atmosphere of trust in which pupils are able to talk freely to one another, and to the teacher, about their own attitudes and assumptions. Such trust is essential in the area of multicultural education which touches on highly controversial issues, about which pupils are likely to be confused and perhaps troubled. Any discussion of racism, for example, is bound to involve sooner or later some consideration of our own attitudes and how these attitudes are related to discriminatory practices within society. Such discussion will remain hopelessly super-ficial unless pupils and teachers can exchange their views frankly and honestly.

This is not to say that teachers should condone racist views, but that they should respect their pupils sufficiently to challenge such views, when they arise, by recourse to reason rather than dogmatic assertion. There is, on the other hand, little point in the teacher adopting a position of academic, or what is sometimes referred to as 'procedural' (Stenhouse, 1983, 133–9), neutrality when confronted with views of this kind. By adopting such a stance teachers risk confusing pupils as to their real intentions. What is needed is a clear statement of principle, backed up by rational argument and relevant information. If these fail to convince, the right to differ should be upheld.

Above all, teachers need to show that they are listening and that they are willing, if necessary, to rethink their own attitudes in the light of the pupils' own insights. In that way dialogue becomes a vehicle for change. There is, after all, no point in asking pupils for their opinions if one is unwilling to respond to what they are saying. Pupils see through such a ploy. They realize that it has little, if anything, to do with genuine collaboration and quickly write it off as a waste of time. Only when honest dialogue is accompanied by a willingness to change does it enable both pupils and teachers to learn together.

This notion of collaborative learning is as relevant to the tutorial as it is to the teaching situation. Indeed, the distinction between these two sets of concerns becomes decidedly blurred when applied to multicultural education: incidents occurring in the playground carry over into the lesson, while work in the classroom may in turn centre on troubled areas of the pupils' own experience. Both the pastoral and curricular aspects of the teaching task, in other words, are determined to some extent by the pupils' need to understand and come to terms with the complex network of social relationships existing inside and outside the school.

An example of the way in which the concerns of the classroom are determined by social factors is to be found in the following extract from a discussion between a primary school teacher and his class about an incident of racist name-calling. Kim had called John a racist name and after talking with the teacher had written a letter of apology:

John:	Usually when it happens you just want to get the person that said it, really.
Teacher:	You were really angry, and shaking and crying weren't you?
Kim:	It weren't really me only that said it, it was Cheryl as well but Cheryl got out of it so I got all the blame.
Teacher:	But what do you feel about the way we dealt with that, was it better or not?
John:	That's the best way to deal with it really. Have a talk with each child and see what you can do and when you can see which one is right or which one wrong let that person who is wrong say they're sorry or whatever . . .
Teacher:	Kim, do you really think you were wrong that time?
Kim:	Yea.
Teacher:	And what did yo think when you wrote the letter to John? Did you *feel* that or were you just doing it because you were told to?
Kim	I weren't doing it because I was told to. I shouldn't have said it in the first place.
Teacher:	What did you think, John, when you got the letter back?
John:	Yes, it's alright but usually you can't take an apology for a few minutes can you? It sticks in your mind . . . Usually you don't like taking a letter you like hearing it personally. Like when Kim gave me the letter I made her read it out to me and say it to me first.
Lorraine:	You know when you tell teachers something. Like if you had a fight, they look at you as if they don't know you, as if you came from Mars or Jupiter or something.
John:	Yes, like you're an outerspacer, like they've never seen you before. (Francis, 1983, 16)

This discussion illustrates, within a practical context, many of the points made earlier about the nature of collaborative learning. There is, for example, a genuine attempt by the teacher to help the pupils explore the attitudes and feelings within the group: 'What did you think . . .?' and 'What did you feel . . .?' are recurring themes in the questions he poses.

Although Kim remains defensive ('It weren't really me only that said it . . .') and, initially, monosyllabic ('Yea') in her response, John takes the opportunity of analysing his own behaviour ('usually you can't take an apology for a few minutes . . .'). This self-appraisal, moreover, extends to the teacher's own attempts to gain feedback on his handling of the situation: 'But what do you feel about the way we dealt with that, was it better or not?' Throughout, he is a prompter; nudging the pupils towards an articulation of their own experience, rather than imposing upon them his own interpretation. 'The vital thing', as Martin Francis (the teacher in question) has himself pointed out, 'is to respect their feelings, because all the time I'm encouraging them to reflect that what they say counts' (quoted in Twitchin and Demuth, 1981, 55).

Although this particular example, unlike the last, is taken from a multiracial school, the kind of sensitive appraisal through discussion which it illustrates is just as necessary in the non-multiracial classroom. Racist jokes and stereotyping, whether they occur in the course of the pupils' own conversations or in the materials that inform the lesson, need confronting. The assumptions underlying them should be questioned and their implications examined. This is particularly so in non-multiracial schools where the stereotypes implicit in racist humour are unchallenged by the presence of minority ethnic groups.

Couched, as they invariably are, in the form of covert invitations to collude, such stereotypes may be extremely difficult to tackle head-on. Indeed, teachers who attempt to do so may all too easily be seen as obsessive killjoys: unable to share in a joke and forever taking the light things seriously. The only way round this problem is to set aside time, as part of the organized tutorial programme, for talks, discussions and workshops aimed at increasing the general level of racism awareness within the school. While complementing the developmental work carried out within the overt curriculum, such a programme would focus specifically on the interpersonal attitudes and individual awareness of pupils. Clearly, it would have to be geared to the particular needs of the group, but might well draw on a range of materials and resources already available. (See, for example, the exercises presented in Judy Katz's (1978) *White Awareness: Handbook for Anti-Racism Training* and Birmingham Education Department's (1982) filmstrip/cassette *Recognising Racism*.)

Neither experiential exercises nor visual aids are of any use, however, if the teachers using them are insensitive to the need for increased racism awareness and unwilling to respond to this need as a team. Professional collaboration between colleagues and collaborative learning in the classroom are mutually dependent: the first is a pointless gesture if unaccompanied by the second; the second is impracticable without the first. Teachers – to return to a theme sounded earlier in this chapter – need support if they are to create within the school the kinds of social relationships which allow for effective anti-racist practice. Such support includes clear leadership from the top and well-defined sanctions against any form of racist behaviour.

THE USE OF SANCTIONS

The question of whether schools should operate sanctions against racist behaviour is a vexed one. There is a strong tendency among teachers to turn a blind eye to the racist nature of certain forms of abuse and aggression. Racist name-calling, for example, is seen as teasing or provocation; racist violence as bullying or fighting. Where these contravene the existing rules of the school they are, of course, condemned. However, there is no recognition of the racist motivation behind the actions and, therefore, no attempt to confront the individuals concerned with their own racism. Even where the racist nature of the actions is recognized, doubts are sometimes expressed as to whether it is in the best interests of the victim to expose the culprit. Thus special sanctions against racist behaviour in schools tend to be seen as either unnecessary or counter-productive.

In schools where such sanctions are considered necessary, teachers have found them to be an effective means of presenting a united front against racism and, thereby, of reducing the number of racist incidents. Sanctions of this kind are not an alternative to collaborative tutorial work, which remains a supremely important area of development. No matter how successful this work may be, however, it cannot compensate for the racism within society. Clear sanctions against racist behaviour are in fact the only means of ensuring a genuine sense of security, within which teachers can begin to educate their pupils for a multicultural society. The crucial question is not 'Shall we?', but *How* shall we?': What form, in other words, should the sanctions take and how can they be most effectively operated?

Tackling this question involves making distinctions between the kinds of racist behaviour to be found in schools. Fortunately, a number of schools have now developed clear guidelines in this area. The following pointers draw particularly on documents produced by Rosendale Junior School (1981) and North Westminster Community School (1982). According to these, a number of problems can be pinpointed, each of which requires a particular pattern of response:

The introduction of racist literature and materials onto the school premises. All schools, regardless of intake and catchment area, are liable to infiltration by racist organizations. The question, as the Berkshire discussion paper makes clear, is: 'What steps should schools take to oppose racialist organisations which attempt to distribute literature, or to gain recruits, amongst their pupils?' (Berkshire Royal County, 1982, 14). Clearly, the refusal to connive with the hiring out of school premises for the meetings of such organizations is an essential step to take. It is also important, however, to take a stand against any pupil who is bringing racist literature and materials into the school or wearing badges and other insigna belonging to these organizations. Pupils should be told that these are not allowed in school and that they might, in the case of literature distributed to other pupils, be confiscated. Offending pupils should be referred to a senior member of staff and the parents informed. Any persistent offender should be excluded from the school until the matter has been fully discussed with the parents of that pupil.

The exclusion of pupils from school activities on racial or cultural grounds. Every pupil should have the right to be included in all school activities. That right, however, may be denied in a number of ways. The school, for example, may inadvertently exclude a pupil from certain activities on cultural or linguistic grounds. Where this is seen to be occurring immediate action should be taken to remedy the situation. On the other hand, the pupils themselves may contribute to the problem by refusing to cooperate with others because of their ethnic group. Obviously, such cases require great sensitivity and tact. Nevertheless, if the problem persists after talking with the pupils, the teacher should refer it to the pastoral head and arrange, if possible, for an interview with the parents.

Verbal abuse or the incitement of others to collaborate in that abuse. Verbal abuse, including name-calling, racial jokes and mimicry, may take place whether or not the victims are present at the time. The North Westminster Community School document is unambiguous in its attitude to such behaviour: 'No member of staff should ignore any form of verbal racist abuse anywhere in the school. It is unacceptable behaviour and must be stopped' (North Westminster Community School, 1982). Clearly, where the jokes or mimicry are not directed at particular members of the school, they may be dealt with through informal discussion. They should, nevertheless, be taken extremely seriously. Where the abuse is directed at a particular person or group within the school, the teacher should explain fully to the culprit and victim that such behaviour will not be tolerated. All such incidents should be recorded and persistent offenders referred to a senior member of staff.

Physical attacks of a racist nature by pupils against other pupils or racist intimidation. Racist intimidation should be treated as seriously as physical assault. There is obviously a problem here, in that the distinction between verbal abuse and intimidation may seem a fine one. The difference, however, is more than just one of degree. Intimidation involves a systematic and premeditated attempt to inspire fear in others, while verbal abuse as understood above includes an element of spontaneity. In categorizing incidents of this sort, teachers have to rely heavily on circumstantial evidence: Was this a single, 'uncharacteristic' incident? Was the exchange conducted in anger? What was its effect on the victim? Where the case is clearly one of intimidation – or where it involves any form of violence – the culprit should be excluded from the school immediately, pending a formal interview with the parents. The purpose of this exclusion is (1) to safeguard the victim, (2) to stress the seriousness of the offence, and (3) to allow the culprit an opportunity to reflect upon the incident and its implications. A record of the attack or intimidation and of the action taken should, of course, be kept by the school.

The involvement of parents is a crucial element in any attempt to deal effectively with the four problem areas mentioned above. This is not to say that the parents will necessarily agree with the stand taken by the school. Indeed, in some cases their views may be as racist as those of the pupil. If they see, however, that the school is firm in its resolve to act against racist behaviour, they are likely to exert a moderating influence on the behaviour of their child. The onus is upon the school to explain its position to the parents and to gain, if possible, their understanding and support.

The fact that these are not always forthcoming is one reason for keeping a full and detailed report of all racist incidents within the school. Teachers need evidence to put before parents, particularly in cases involving pupils who are persistent offenders. They also need, for their own benefit, to be able to track trends and patterns in racist behaviour among pupils. Very little is known about the workings of racism as it effects the social relationships within the school. The collection of evidence can help teachers understand it more fully and thereby explain it more clearly to the parents on whose support they must rely.

One school at least has made a start on trying to understand the extent and nature of racist opinion among pupils. The staff of Quintin Kynaston School distinguishes between 'hard-core racists' and 'students on the periphery': of the former, 'some . . . are openly and vocally abusive of blacks/Asians while others mutter inaudible jibes and comments in the presence of minority groups or of staff members, or secretly write racist graffiti around the school'; the latter 'make occasional racist comments but their abuse is a spontaneous and individual expression unlike the collective jargon of the hard-core racists'. A further category, according to the staff members, includes 'misguided or unintentional racists, who put forward their belief (often "politely") that "immigrants" are responsible for the present crisis in unemployment and housing' (Quintin Kynaston School, 1982). While effective pastoral work can never be reduced to the simple expedient of relating individual attitudes to a broad, prespecified typology, the empirically observed patterns of behaviour noted in the Quintin Kynaston document can be useful to teachers who have to deal with pupils involved in incidents of racist abuse and violence. It is, for example, usually possible to appeal to pupils' 'on the periphery' by talking to them after class. The 'hard-core racist', however, is likely to require much stiffer sanctions.

While of the three groups the 'misguided or unintentional

racists' are most likely to respond positively to education programmes designed to promote racial tolerance, they present a particular problem. Partly this problem is that their racism may be well disguised and therefore difficult to confront; partly, also, that many teachers, as the Rampton Report spells out, are themselves 'unintentional racists' (Department of Education and Science, 1981) and may, unwittingly or otherwise, confirm such pupils in their racist views. No school can afford, when considering racialist behaviour, to overlook the racism among its own staff. This is likely to span as broad a spectrum as among the pupils, but will manifest itself in very different ways. Those teachers who are members of, say, the National Front will almost certainly not advertise the fact in school. Nor are racist abuse and violence potential problems among teachers. The real problem is to be found in a general unwillingness among teachers to admit that racism exists and that schools should, and can, take a positive and effective stand against it. This unwillingness, if not racist in itself, is certainly a collusion with racism.

CROSS-CULTURAL COUNSELLING

By way of conclusion to this chapter I shall discuss briefly an aspect of the teacher's pastoral role that has received scant attention within educational circles: cross-cultural counselling. In doing so I shall, inevitably, be narrowing the focus of attention onto the concerns of those teachers who work in a multiracial context. For those who work in other settings, however, this section may still have some relevance, since the problem it poses is common to a wide range of situations. The estrangement of teachers from the cultural world of their pupils is by no means limited to the multiracial school.

The problem of estrangement is particularly acute in counselling, the core of which, according to Colin Lago, is the attempt 'to understand the client as if one were the client' (Lago, 1981, 62). From the 'client's', or in our case the pupil's, point of view this process offers what the British Association for Counselling (BAC) refers to as an 'opportunity to explore, discover and clarify ways of living more resourcefully and towards greater well-being' (British Association for Counselling, 1979). Counselling, so conceived, is the art of listening.

Disciplined listening of this kind is never an easy matter.

When conducted in a multiracial context it may present the teacher with what has been described as an 'almost impossible task' (Lago and Ball, 1983, 39). The disparity of experience between the counsellor and pupil in certain cross-cultural encounters poses a crucial question: How, as a white teacher, can I begin to understand the black pupil 'as if' I were that pupil, when I have had no experience of what it is to be a victim of racial prejudice and discrimination?

One answer to that question is simply 'You can't!': 'no matter how well-founded the intentions, there's no way a white man can ever know what it's like to live in a black skin' (Rack, 1978, 133). For the practising teacher any such denial will seem somewhat academic. The white teacher attempting to counsel the black pupil must, in practice, cling to the possibility that a wary, sympathetic imagination will win through. This is not to deny the importance of the black British person's self-determination, but simply to acknowledge the demands of the teacher's many-sided role. A more pragmatic response, then, is to admit that any attempt at cross-cultural counselling is fraught with difficulties, and to go on from there to try to understand more clearly what these difficulties are.

A large part of the problem in any cross-cultural encounter is ensuring that you are hearing what the pupil intends you to hear. The cultural differences between people of differing ethnic backgrounds may stretch the counsellor's skill in active, interpretive listening to its limit. These cultural differences include distinct patterns, not only of verbal and non-verbal behaviour, but of the social conventions governing each:

Verbal behaviour. Difficultues may arise over the meaning of particular words and phrases; as in the case of the Creole speaker, for whom the expression, 'Mind you don't go home,' means the exact opposite of what it means to the speaker of standard English. Other difficulties may centre on the intonation patterns employed by various speakers. By placing the emphases on different parts of the sentence, the speaker for whom English is a second language may, for example, communicate to an 'English as mother tongue' speaker a tone or attitude that is quite unintended.

Non-verbal behaviour. An example which illustrates the extent to which apparently minor aspects of non-verbal behaviour can affect our assessment of individuals comes from a recent report which found that half of the Asian student doctors taking an important Royal College examination were failing it because of their pattern of eye contact. Their avoidance of eye contact with their examiners throughout the examination was misinterpreted as diffidence, or even shiftiness, by those for whom it was intended as a mark of respect. The consequences of this misinterpretation, as far as the teachers' career prospects were concerned, were disastrous (Ezard, 1983).

Social conventions. Difficulties may also centre on what is felt to be appropriate within the counselling situation. Colin Lago has suggested, for example, that 'whereas for an Englishman it may be appropriate to ask reasonably direct questions early in an interview, such directness, to an Asian interviewee, would be interpreted as most impolite' (Lago, 1981, 61). The point was made more strongly by a group of third-year Bengali girls in an east London comprehensive school. When asked, in the course of a class discussion, where they might go for help and advice if they needed it, one of the pupils replied: 'We wouldn't. We don't want our inside problems to go out.'

A crucial step towards overcoming the kinds of difficulties mentioned above is simply to acknowledge that, in cross-cultural counselling, there will almost certainly be aspects of each person's style of communication that the other is unaware of; to be sensitive, in other words, to the fact that 'we don't know what we don't know' about the other person's communicative intent. To discover what these areas of ignorance are, and how they affect the counselling task, requires a willingness on behalf of the counsellor to learn something of the child's cultural background. It is not, however, an abstract or academic knowledge that is needed – although books may help – but a personal knowledge that comes from genuine dialogue.

In cross-cultural counselling, as in any other kind of counselling, teachers must feel their way, acquiring the necessary skills and expertise as they proceed. There is a danger in prespecifying, as Douglas Hamblin (after Rogers, 1951, and Truax and Carkhuff, 1967) has done, 'the personality of the counsellor' (Hamblin, 1974, 11–14). Julian Wohl (1976) has suggested, for example, that the qualities of genuineness, warmth and empathy, as initially defined by Rogers (1951), are inappropriate in counselling situations involving people of Burmese origin, who might rate them as evidence of weakness and incompetence on the part of the counsellor. Insofar as the notion of 'the personality of the counsellor' is a useful one, it should be seen as denoting a product as well as a prerequisite of effective pastoral work in schools.

There is an equal danger, however, of oversensitivity. The teacher who, as Paul Zec put it, 'approaches cultural differences as something "given" and not to be, as it were, tampered with . . . provides logical support for just that which people most concerned with multicultural education abhor – stereotyping of pupils by teachers' (Zec, 1981, 42–3). To be effective pastorally, teachers need to be sure about the general principles – such as that of respect for persons – which guide their work. Without a keen awareness of their own cultural framework and a sense of confidence in the educational values to which they adhere, teachers are unlikely to be of much use to their pupils. For it is only possible to understand a pupil 'as if' one were that pupil, by first finding out what it is in oneself that has to be bracketed in order to achieve that understanding. Counselling has nothing to do with self-surrender.

Nor does it have to do with imposing one's own preconceptions on the pupil. Only by approaching the other person with great tact and circumspection can the counsellor avoid stereotyping the pupil. Although the identity of minority ethnic groups in Britain is shaped by their members' common experience of racial discrimination and prejudice, each such group contains within it great diversity of attitude and opinion. Counsellors who rely on the traditional culture of a particular group as their only reference point will be unaware of the adaptations which many immigrant groups have already made. They will also be insensitive to the situation of those born in Britain who are forming a distinct culture of their own, different from both that of their parents and that of white society. For counsellors who want to see beyond the stereotypes, the most authoritative primary source must be the case in front of them.

In an article to which I have already referred, Colin Lago and Russell Ball offer what they describe as 'some tentative guidelines for those involved in cross-cultural counselling'. These sum up many of the points mentioned in this section. The following items from their checklist are essential starting points for any teachers trying to develop their counselling skills within a multicultural context:

- To have a genuine interest in and knowledge of the client's culture.
- To develop awareness of one's own cultural framework and how this may differ from that of the client.
- To attempt to gain knowledge of the moral values of the other culture.
- To be aware of our own cultural norms about verbal and non-verbal communication.
- The counsellor needs to have security within his own cultural identity and personality to risk exploring in the client's cultural framework and yet not get lost in it.
- The counsellor needs to consider carefully many ethical concepts, including confidentiality, his role in the situation, his underlying philosophy, all of which may have very different connotations for the client.
- In some complex situations a model of minimum intervention may be appropriate.
- To develop knowledge of when it may be appropriate to refer people to other forms of help, possibly from their own cultures, and try to build a network of such provision. (Lago and Ball, 1983, 48)

That last item is a reminder of what has been one of the major themes of the present chapter: the need for a collaborative base to the social relationships within the school and education service as a whole. Unless that base is strengthened and, where possible, extended into the local community and wider educational context, teachers will find themselves in an increasingly isolated position and without the support necessary for effective developmental work. Building what Lago and Ball refer to as a 'network of provision' is a prerequisite, not only of cross-cultural counselling, but of every aspect of multicultural education. Without such provision, the education service will remain parochial, both in its concerns and in its practices.

This chapter has tried to show that multicultural education does not develop in a social vacuum. It is a product of certain kinds of social relationships as well as particular forms of curriculum planning. The quality of the relationships within any school depends, it has been argued, upon three factors: (1) the degree of collaboration between colleagues; (2) the value placed on collaborative learning in the classroom; and (3) the existence of clear sanctions against any form of racist behaviour. Finally, a number of issues relating to the task of counselling in a multicultural setting have been raised and the need for teachers to rethink their counselling role in the light of these issues has been stressed. The question of social relationships – and their impact on the education of pupils in and for a multicultural society – continues to be of central importance as we turn, in the next chapter, to the more practical concerns of the classroom.

CHAPTER FIVE

Classroom Approaches

Multicultural education, as defined in the previous pages, leads beyond an exclusive concern with the personal experience of pupils and teachers to a more informed consideration of the wider implications of living in a racist society. No single classroom approach is adequate to this task. What is needed is a critical examination of the existing approaches, in order that the limitations and potential of each can be appreciated and a coordinated strategy developed. The present chapter attempts such an examination, using as its point of reference the general curriculum aims outlined at the end of chapter 2. These aims, it is argued, can only be realized through a composite programme whereby the strengths of one approach are used to compensate for the weaknesses of another.

AWARENESS OF RACISM

The term 'race relations teaching' has in the past been used to describe programmes of work developed within the context of the British curriculum research and development movement in an attempt to raise pupils' awareness of racism in contemporary society (see, for example, Sikes, 1979). More recently, however, the phrase 'racism awareness', imported originally from the USA, has gained considerable currency in this country (see, for example, Ruddell, 1983). It was used in the previous chapter with specific reference to the pastoral curriculum. Its relevance, as we shall see, also extends to the overt curriculum where it pinpoints a significant growth point in current classroom practice.

A criticism to which this perspective lays itself open is that it places undue stress on the notion of racism as individual prejudice. This may be the case in certain instances, but is not necessarily so. Certainly, the examples offered in the following pages emphasize the institutional effects of racial discrimination as well as the personal effects of racial prejudice. They also stress the need for a firm anti-racist stance by the teachers concerned. Those who adopt and declare such a value position within the classroom sometimes choose to refer to their work as 'anti-racist teaching'. The following examples assume a firm commitment by teachers to such a stance.

Direct approach

Broadly speaking there are two approaches to 'racism awareness' teaching. The first of these I refer to as the 'direct approach' because it makes explicit reference to racism and explores specific instances of racist practice. It is often assumed that this approach is unsuitable for younger children. In my own experience this is not the case. The one essential requirement governing its use is that the teacher should have achieved a good working relationship with the group and that the pupils should be capable of sustaining frank and open discussions with one another. Given such conditions, which may well take some time to develop, there is no reason why pupils of any age cannot benefit from this approach.

Although cross-curricular in its application, the direct approach relies heavily on certain teaching methods; in particular, small-group discussion and role-play. Both these methods need grounding in carefully chosen materials if they are to give rise to an informed consideration of the wider social issues. Unless an attempt is made to inform the work in this way, pupils are restricted to their own received opinions. Under such circumstances small-group discussion and role-play may serve to confirm, rather than combat, the racial prejudice within the group. Given appropriate materials, however, these methods can be an effective means of enabling pupils to clarify their own frame of values.

A first-year lesson, taught within the context of a general humanities course, provides a useful example of the way in which materials can be used, both as a means of achieving a focus and as an informing device. At the start of this lesson the teacher handed each pupil an extract from a brief autobiographical account by Linette Simms, who had migrated to Britain from Jamaica in 1953. Part of this extract read as follows:

When I came here I remember it was a winter night and I landed at Plymouth. I didn't have any address to go to. I didn't have any friends, no one to meet me and it was night when the boat landed there. I didn't know where to turn. But I remember going to a policeman and saying to him, 'Good evening. Can you help me? I arrived in this country and I haven't got anywhere to go.' He said, 'I beg your pardon.' I said, 'I haven't got anyone to meet me. I haven't got anywhere to go.' He said, 'Why you come here then?' I said, 'To seek employment.' There was another passenger on the same ship who heard me talking to the police, a West Indian lady. And she said to me, 'Oh, I heard you talking on the ship that you haven't got anyone to meet you. But I didn't think you were serious. You can come with me. My uncle has got a room provided for me.' Just like that. This officer said to her, 'Are you sure?' She said, 'Yes, she can come with me.' And I went home with her and we shared this room together.

Her relatives got both of us a job the following morning, straight away. My first job was in a tea shop in Piccadilly. My wages was £3.12.6d per week. Out of that I paid my fares to work, my rent, and look after myself, save. Two or three years after I sent for my father. (Fyson and Greenhill, 1979, 3)

The advantage of this extract was that it presented the pupils with a clearly defined situation and a cental character with which they could easily identify. Personal testimony of this kind, because of its immediacy and direct appeal, is always a useful way of introducing unfamiliar roles and situations. The task the pupils were given on this occasion was to discuss and write down the problems they thought Linette Simms might have encountered on her first day at work. After a brief reporting-back session these problems were used as a basis for a role-playing exercise in which the pupils recreated the 'tea shop in Piccadilly' and Linette's first day there.

This phase of the lesson was followed by a discussion in which the pupils were asked to imagine what Linette's life might have been like several years later. A further role-playing exercise was structured round a fictional situation in which she and her friend go to eat in a restaurant. Having acted out this situation the pupils were handed copies of a report which appeared in the *Daily Mirror* during 1965 under the headline 'No coloureds, said the Chinese waiter'. This report began as follows:

> The Jamaican couple had just sat down in the Chinese restaurant. Then, according to a customer, a Chinese waiter came up and said: 'I'm sorry – we do not serve coloured people here.' Now the customer, Mr Frank Johnson, who claims that he saw this incident while he was eating in the restaurant, has sent a letter of complaint to the town's mayor.
>
> Mr Johnson said yesterday: 'I was disgusted. The place went deadly quiet. Like myself, people were upset. It was shocking to treat any human being like that.'
>
> He said the incident happened in the Oi Kun Restaurant in Wolverhampton. (*Daily Mirror*, 1965, 4)

In groups of three or four the pupils discussed the report and compared it with what had happened in the previous role-playing exercise that they had participated in. One group related the incident to the treatment Linette Simms said she had received at the hands of the policeman on first arrival in Plymouth. Another group talked about whether an incident like the one reported in the newspaper could still happen today. A further group wondered why the newspaper had selected this particular incident of racial discrimination and whether Mr Johnson would have responded with such indignation if it had been an English restaurant. Throughout this small-group discussion period the pupils were using the material as a means of consolidating the work they had done, exchanging personal anecdotes and stories, and gently challenging one another's views and assumptions.

Indirect approach

There are a number of reasons why teachers may choose not to use a direct approach to racism awareness teaching. They may, for example, feel that they have insufficient time with a group to create the necessary social cohesion within which a serious exploration of racism might be possible. Or they may feel that they themselves are not as yet ready to confront controversial issues of this kind with their pupils. In such cases an alternative is to approach these issues indirectly, by way of analogous situations or generalized themes and topics which may suggest the more specific issue of racism without necessarily making it explicit.

The problem with such an approach, as any teacher who has ever tried to organize topic work will be aware, is that it not only reduces the teacher's control over the focus of the work, but also offers few clues as to the kinds of connections the pupils are making between the general theme and the specific issue. The teacher, in other words, can never be sure that an unstated link or an implicit analogy has been fully grasped by the pupils. This problem is particularly acute since the point of this approach is to allow them to explore the issue of racism at their own pace and in their own way. Any attempt by the teacher to make explicit the links, or to pry too pointedly into the pupils' understanding of them, may well frustrate this urge towards greater pupil autonomy.

This impasse to which the indirect approach may lead is a very serious drawback. An advantage of the approach, on the other hand, is that it is particularly well suited to interdisciplinary styles of work, where skills and information from various subject areas can feed into the general topic. It is this tilt towards an interdisciplinary perspective, rather than the relevance of the approach to a specific age group, that makes it appropriate for use in the primary school. For the potential of integrated schemes of work has been much more fully realized in the early years of schooling than it has in the secondary sector.

An example of such a scheme is to be found in the account, already quoted in the opening chapter, that Sylvia Collicott gives of a series of lessons in which she approached the theme of migration by way of the pupils' own experience of moving house. In this instance the indirect approach allowed the teacher to introduce the pupils to certain general categories which they were later able to apply to the theme of migration. This strategy is by no means restricted to the primary school, but can be used to good effect with older pupils. The secondary school art teacher, for example, might well employ the indirect approach when helping pupils to examine their own experience of colour: What associations do certain colours carry? Does colour carry its own coded messages? If so, do the colour codes vary from culture to culture? Questions such as this might be expected to nudge pupils towards a greater degree of awareness concerning their own prejudices and presuppositions.

The indirect approach is severely limited, but is nevertheless better than nothing. It can barely begin to inform pupils about the reality of institutional racism, since it fails by design to make that reality explicit. It can, however, sensitize pupils to their own prejudices and, if handled with skill, provide them with general categories that may prove useful in any later analysis of racism in contemporary society. Ideally, it would always be seen as a prelude to the direct approach or to one of the other approches to which we shall now turn.

MINORITIES IN BRITAIN

An exclusive concern with either the direct or indirect approaches to racism awareness teaching runs the risk of presenting a stereotyped view of minority ethnic groups as the helpless victims of racism. The sensitive and skilful teacher can avoid such a presentation by highlighting instances of resistance to racism within contemporary society. A further perspective is also needed, however, by which pupils are able to see members of such groups as capable of exercising self-determination and agency. Approaches which emphasize the strengths of cultural diversity — both in historical and contemporary terms — are crucial in this respect.

The term 'black studies' has in the past been used to denote this particular perspective. The trouble with this term for our purposes is that it suggests the development of a discrete curriculum unit rather than the permeation of the whole curriculum with new insights and subject matter. Nevertheless, the two approaches which I shall discuss in association with this perspective have their roots in the 'black studies' movement as it developed in the USA and, later, in England. A criticism that is sometimes levelled against this movement is that it is based upon a naive celebration of culture. Although not entirely unjustified, this criticism is less applicable in the case of the more recent developments discussed in the following pages. The purpose of both the positive approach and the black British history approach is not to celebrate, but simply to reclaim, histories and cultures which have previously been either denied, distorted or just ignored.

Positive approach

In attempting to build upon the strengths of cultural diversity, both within the local community and within the wider context of British society, the positive approach can be used in either the multiracial or non-multiracial classroom. It is likely to operate differently, however, in each of these settings. An example of its use in the multiracial classroom is to be found in Hilary Claire's account of a project called 'Memories'. She developed this project with a class of nine- and ten-year-olds which includes pupils whose families originated from Cyprus, Somalia, Malta, Nigeria, Morocco, China and Vietnam (Claire, 1983).

The project was designed to give the pupils an opportunity of 'sharing stories about life in other countries, about feelings of leaving one's country, as well as personal stories about childhood'. This exploration of the children's own experience and that of their families would, the teacher hoped, 'make world events accessible to them' and 'start them thinking about international events' by relating these to their own and their peers' lives (ibid., 14). The aim was to enable the pupils to learn from one another's experience and to prompt them to critical thought about that experience.

Much of the first session was spent round a table, the teacher and pupils talking together about their earliest memories. Each child was then given a large piece of sugar paper. These were folded into eight sections so that the pupils could record important events and memories sequentially. The teacher made it clear that they did not necessarily have to think of something for every year of their lives, but that each of them should aim to record as full and detailed a personal history as possible. In preparation for the next session the pupils were to ask their parents, older siblings, aunts, uncles, grandparents or whoever to tell them about some of the important events that had happened in their families, about why they had moved from their original homes, and about their own babyhood.

As a way of informing the work further the teacher sent a

letter, translated where necessary, explaining to all parents that the pupils were doing a project on their personal histories and memories and asking for the parents' help. In response to this letter several children came to school with stories told them by their parents and with family photographs. The children's enthusiasm, and the quality of the writing and art work they produced, convinced the teacher 'that working in this way is likely to be highly productive in the multicultural classroom, even where there isn't such a range of unique experience' (Claire, 1983, 15).

Nevertheless, the success of this work did rely upon the wide diversity of cultural backgrounds represented within the classroom. This in itself limited the application of the approach. No such limitation is attached to Ray Hemmings' attempts to develop the positive approach in relation to mathematics teaching in both primary and secondary schools. In two extremely useful articles (Hemmings, 1980a and b) he has shown how the products of different cultures may provide the most effective means of imparting certain mathematical concepts. The patterns found in Islamic decorative art, for example, may offer older pupils in particular an introduction to a wide variety of geometric systems. Or an awareness of the subtleties of symmetrical relationships may be developed in younger pupils through the creation of rangoli patterns, those often intricate designs which are used by Hindu and Sikh families to decorate their homes on important occasions. Such activities rely, not upon the divertisy of experience within the group, but upon the variety of material introduced into the lesson by the teacher. They are, therefore, of particular value in the non-multiracial classroom.

The same is certainly true of activities relating to the study of myths. In one form or another such study involves most children and many teachers at various points in the curriculum. Classical studies, religious studies, as well as topics relating to general humanities or integrated courses, frequently contain at least a unit on Graeco-Roman myths and might well be expanded to contain a non-European element. The Hindu notion of 'karma' and Urdu 'qismat', for example, might be usefully compared with the concepts of 'fortuna' and 'ananke' in the Graeco-Roman view of existence. The Schools Council (1977) materials were particularly useful in relating such cross-cultural comparisons to the work of the specialist religious studies teacher. However, the relevance to other subject areas of the comparative study of myths ought not to be overlooked.

Black British history approach

'In 1555', according to the historian Folarin Shyllon, 'five Africans were brought into Britain. Over the next century, more and more Africans were imported. By the middle of the seventeenth century at least, a thriving black community had been established and Britain had ceased to be a white man's country' (Shyllon, 1977, 3). The history of black people in Britain – presented most notably by Shyllon (1974 and 1977) and Scobie (1972) and made accessible through classroom resource books such as those produced by Dodgson (1984), File and Power (1981), and the Institute of Race Relations (1982) – is concerned with the roots of racism and the black response to it. This response, as each of these texts amply illustrates, was 'positive, vibrant, and defiant' (Shyllon, 1977, 3).

Clearly, we are dealing here with a narrower curriculum focus than in the case of the positive approach, which, as we saw, is cross-curricular in its application. The black British history approach is not, however, restricted to the work of history teachers. Moreover, it represents a significant advance on the positive approach, in that it locates the experience of black people in Britain within a broader political, as well as historical, context. Black British history, as presented within this pedagogic tradition, is the record of a positive urge towards liberation and emancipation. It stresses the strengths of diversity, while recognizing that the existence of such diversity depends upon a historic struggle against racism.

Much of the work in this area centres on individuals: Dr Johnson's servant, 'Frank' Barker, for example; the abolitionist, Olaudah Equiano; or the notable figure in the Crimean War, Mary Seacole. Inevitably, our knowledge of many of these figures is based upon secondary sources. In the person of Mary Seacole, however, we are presented with a woman whose personal history not only crossed many of the major public events of her time, but is documented in her recently reissued autobiography (Alexander and Dewjee, 1984). Raising as it does questions concerning the roots of racism and sexism in British society, such a work provides an invaluable source of material for use across a range of subject areas.

The more recent history of the black British can claim a rich tradition of narrative and verse dealing specifically with the experience of migration. Moreover, much of this work is ideally suited to younger readers: Buchi Emecheta's (1974) novel, *Second-Class Citizen*, for example, which reflects her own experience of migration from Lagos to London, or Samuel Selvon's (1956) account in *The Lonely Londoners* of Caribbean people in England during the 1950s. George Lamming's and Edward Brathwaite's work is more demanding but, given judicious selection by the teacher, the black experience of migration as recorded in *The Emigrants* (Lamming, 1980) and *The Arrivants* (Brathwaite, 1973) is accessible to younger pupils.

There is a danger, of course, in conceiving of this approach to multicultural education simply in terms of an injection of new materials into the school curriculum. Where this occurs the complexity of black British history is likely to be minimalized and the image of black people sentimentalized. The subject-matter, therefore, needs to be organized around key concepts, problems and skills. The assumptions underlying such terms as 'civilization' and 'the age of discovery' should be re-examined with the pupils so that they gradually acquire the wherewithal to challenge the ethnocentrism of traditional British history in the light of new evidence and alternative perspectives.

The primary sources that are reproduced in Nigel File's and Chris Power's (1981) *Black Settlers in Britain 1555–1958* are invaluable in this respect. They give pupils the opportunity of studying history at first hand, gaining confidence in reading historical documents, and making their own judgements from the evidence in front of them. For example, pupils might be given copies of the documents relating to the attempt in 1786 by the Committee for the Relief of the Black Poor, comprising a number of prominent businessmen and politicians, to ship the black poor of Britain to Sierra Leone on the west coast of Africa. These documents include an extract from the minutes of the committee showing the age range, qualifications, areas of origin and occupations of the eight members of the black community who were recruited to encourage others to sign up for the scheme (File and Power, 1981, 31). From the information given in this document pupils can think about why these men in particular were considered suitable for the task and how their involvement made it easier for the committee members to present themselves as philanthropists. Through this kind of documentary analysis pupils can begin to understand how racism actually operates in history.

A GLOBAL PERSPECTIVE

'Multi-ethnic education', as David Hicks has pointed out, 'is not just about groups in the United Kingdom. It must also be aware of minority groups elsewhere in the world' (Hicks, 1979, 5). If this is the case, then other classroom approaches are required which offer the kind of global perspective suggested by Hicks. The study of black British history, in other words, needs to be complemented by the study of world history, while the presentation of Britain as a multicultural and multiracial society needs to be set in its international context.

A number of well-established movements within education offer such a perspective. These include 'world studies', 'international education', 'peace studies' and 'development education'. The problem with each of these terms is that they are as heavily contested as is the term 'multicultural education'. The following imaginary case study, produced some years ago by Thomas Cullinan, shows for example how attitudes and ideas within 'development education' have undergone considerable change in the last 25 years:

> In 1960 Sebastian first met up with Oxfam when it was a grotty *charity* in a few rooms in Queen Street. He wanted to help people dying of hunger, help give them food, cash and clothing.
>
> In 1963 he began to see that giving people things in their hunger was not an answer. Indeed, in some ways it made things worse. What he needed was concern for *development*, to help people to feed themselves.
>
> In 1966 he was quite shaken when he realised that the people who harvested the coffee he drank every day lived at starvation level and the man who mined the tin in which the coffee came earned £7 a month in a Bolivian tin mine and warded off hunger by chewing cocoa leaves. Sebastian stopped talked about charity and started talking about *justice*.
>
> In 1969 he came to see that the injustice done against so many destitute people was not just a simple injustice

between groups of people in the world. He came to see it as *structural injustice* . . .

In 1972 Sebastian moved to a further level of response. He began to see that what was really at stake was not people's hunger for more money, food or health, but their hunger for life, for freedom and culture. He saw that the profoundest form of underdevelopment and of oppression is the moral state of men who have sapped out of them any desire to shape their own history . . . He saw that this was the ultimate injustice of man against man. It is roughly what the Latin American thinkers and theologians mean by *liberation* and is quite a shift from some of the ways we tend to think. (Centre for World Development Education, 1979, 50)

If one were to update this scenario and project 'Sebastian' into the 1980s one would no doubt find him reacting against the liberalism of his previously held position and listening in to the current debate on 'whether or not the problem facing world society can be solved within the framework of capitalism' (Hatcher, 1983, 31).

World studies approach

The world studies approach is concerned with improving pupils' understanding of the contemporary world system. Certain key concepts play an important part in any attempt to grasp the complexity of this system: the notion of 'the development of underdevelopment', for example, of 'interdependence' and of 'global inequality'. Pupils are introduced to different ways of classifying the world and are presented with different models for explaining the structure of inequality and the various forms of power that operate internationally. Clearly, geography has a strong claim to a position of central importance in this area. Increasingly, however, a concern with the key concepts of world studies is reflected across a range of subject areas.

In order for such cross-curricular developments to occur, teachers must be willing to redefine the parameters of their own specialisms. The world studies approach, like the other approaches already considered, involves more than an infusion of new subject matter into an old curriculum framework. It leads, rather, to a radical rethink of pedagogical principles. Science education, for example, can offer an ideal opportunity for pupils to discuss in an informed context the implications of the worldwide energy crisis; provided, that is, that science teachers see their role as being to raise issues of value as well as transmit matters of fact. Unless they are willing to extend their role in this way, science teachers become in effect technical instructors. A science with no regard for human values is no science at all.

The same is certainly true of work within the arts and humanities. Clearly, the thrust of the world studies approach as far as religious education is concerned is a greater stress on the study of world religions rather than an exclusive concern with the Christian faith. In fact, however, a serious study of Christianity, or perhaps of any faith, necessarily raises questions about the historical and philosophical relations it bears towards other religions. As a notable German theologian has put it:

> The first schism in the history of the kingdom of God began with the separation between Christianity and Judaism. Even if we are not free to annul that first schism all by ourselves, we can still overcome its fateful effects and arrive at the common ground crossed by paths which are indeed still divided but which none the less run parallel to one another. (Moltmann, 1981, XV)

Jurgen Moltmann is simply affirming here the self-evident truth that the historical Jesus of the Christian faith was always a Jew. He remains, as a contemporary Cambridge theologian has it, 'a sort of Jewish Socrates' (Cupitt, 1979, 68). As such his teachings and his life, as they are presented in the New Testament, sound important themes that are central to Judaism and, arguably, to the other main religions of the world.

Within the arts a global perspective is no less important. Such a perspective, however, should not be seen as a means of merely providing a few examples of different art forms and cultural artifacts. 'Look at Third World art superficially', Brian Allison has insisted, 'and you will be momentarily entertained; respond to it deeply and sensitively and you will permanently expand your concept of art and aesthetic experience' (Allison, 1981, 8). The kinds of understanding that might emerge from a serious and prolonged study of the art of Asia, Africa and Latin America have been specified by Allison in the following terms:

(a) the ways different cultures embody and communicate their beliefs in the visual symbols they produce;
(b) the sources of imagery and symbolism, and that these sources vary from the ritualistic, mythical and magical to representations of visual responses to the environment;
(c) the variety of ways art forms or symbols to be found in a culture influence the lives of the people in that culture;
(d) the ways in which the art forms and materials used in different cultures influence, and are influenced by, the particular kinds of imagery and symbolism;
(e) the ways in which both the art critic and anthropologist can help in providing ways of understanding the art forms of different cultures;
(f) the differing criteria which need to be employed in responding to, comparing and contasting the art forms of different cultures;
(g) the ways artists in one culture derive symbols and images from the art forms of other cultures and attach new meanings to them. (ibid.)

A further important aspect of the world studies approach is an emphasis on learning about the contemporary world economy: trading relationships between the first and third worlds, for example, and the role of the multinational companies, the IMF, the UN, and the main aid agencies. The impact of these trading relationships on the patterns of migration in the post-1945 world is also directly relevant to the world studies approach: the north African and south European migration to the EEC countries, for example, and the Latin American migration to he USA. Insofar as the world studies approach is concerned with understanding how the contemporary world system operates to sustain global inequality, the question of how resources are monopolized, capital created, and labour bought and sold is of vital significance.

World history approach

Clearly, there is a historical dimension to this question which cannot be ignored. The origins of the world economy are to be found in the history of European colonization. Pupils require at the very least a brief survey of this history if they are to acquire an understanding of the relationship between industrialization and empire and the kinds of ideological justifications that have been given in support of this relationship. Seen in this light the world history approach is a direct complement to the world studies approach. It enables pupils to understand the origins of global inequality, the roots of racism, and the history of radical resistance by minority groups throughout the world.

The work of the history department at Villiers High School in Southall serves as a useful example of this approach. The course offered to pupils during their first three years at the school is skills-based and thematic, focusing upon such topics as the nature of evidence in historical enquiry, peoples on the move and migration, and social and political change. Within the broad thematic framework certain events and episodes are examined in detail. These include the Amritsar massacre instigated by General Dyer in 1911, the partition of India in 1947, and the explusion of the Ugandan Asians by Idi Amin in 1972.

Where possible the material for this course draws on the cultural resources of the local community. Thus, for example, the unit on the partition of India makes use of an interview with a member of the local community who was born and brought up in India, lived through the partition, and subsequently migrated to Britain. In examining the transcript of this interview pupils are asked to test the validity of this record against the available documentary evidence and other eye-witness accounts. The stress throughout is on pupils developing a historical sense through exercising their critical judgement. Given the inherent bias of much of the secondary source material in this area, the use of primary sources together with the development of a critical attitude towards these sources is a major feature of the world history approach.

Literature and art work provide a further invaluable, if neglected, means of achieving a less Eurocentric view of history. They can also form the basis for a useful interchange of ideas between history and English specialists and those working in the arts. Grace Nichols' epic poem, *I is a Long Memoried Woman* (Nichols, 1983), serves as an example of the kind of material that can extend the understanding of both pupils and teachers alike. Spanning the experience of an African woman uprooted through slavery to Caribbean soil, the poem, as the following extract shows, is concerned with the disintegrating force of the colonial experience and the solidarity and endurance of the women:

> We the women who toil
> unadorn
> heads tie with cheap
> cotton
>
> We the women who cut
> clear fetch dig sing
>
> We the women making
> something from this
> ache-and-pain-a-me
> back-o-hardness
>
> Yet we the women
> who praises go unsung
> who voices go unheard
> who deaths they sweep
> aside
> as easy as dead leaves
>   (ibid., 13)

The value of such material is that it is accessible without ever talking down to its readers; that it is informed by a deep understanding of its subject-matter; and that its author, a Guyanese writer, is herself part of the history she relates. Perspective is all important here. Since the purpose of this approach is to offer an alternative to the traditional Eurocentric view so often adopted in classroom textbooks, it is essential that the materials reflect the colonial experience from the standpoint of the colonized. This means that teachers who want to push forward the boundaries of the curriculum on this front must be willing to research the field afresh and, if necessary, develop their own materials and resources.

A COMPOSITE STRATEGY

The foregoing outline is not intended to be a comprehensive overview. The aim has been to show the complementarity of certain clearly bounded, though overlapping, pedagogic approaches currently being used in schools. None of these approaches is adequate on its own. What is needed is a composite strategy whereby the strengths of one approach counterbalance the weaknesses, and reinforce the strengths, of another; whereby, for example, the emphasis on racism as a contemporary reality, which is implicit in the direct approach, reinforces the stress within the black British history approach on the roots of racism and the historic resistance to racism by the black community in Britain. Combined in this way the various approaches can act as a system of checks and balances against the limitations of a single approach. The crucial question for the teacher is how to coordinate these approaches – in what curricular combinations, with what colleagues, and using what resources – in such a way as to provide an effective cross-curricular response.

Since any answer to this question necessarily depends on the circumstances pertaining in specific schools, no single solution can be offered. It is possible, however, to pinpoint certain paired priorities. These are, unfortunately, all too often presented as alternatives. Thus, racism awareness teaching is set against teaching about cultural diversity; experiential learning against the learning of facts and skills; a contemporary perspective against a historical; local issues against universal. Forcing distinctions in this way is a time-honoured method of scoring academic points. Yet, judged against the need for a coordinated response to racism in British schools, this kind of 'either/or' analysis is not only false but positively harmful. Schools seriously attempting such a response would do well to adopt a policy of pedagogical eclecticism which would allow them to transform, at the level of classroom practice, the 'either/or' into a 'both/and'.

Racism awareness and *teaching about diversity*. The notions of racism and of cultural diversity are closely related. One makes little sense without the other. Pupils need to know about the histories, customs and life-styles of particular minority groups if they are to understand how racism has worked, and continues to work, in practice. Similarly, they need some conceptual grasp of the idea of racism as an ideology and as a set of institutional practices if their understanding of cultural diversity is to have any intellectual rigour. In effect this means that teachers should make use of both the direct approach to racism awareness and the positive and black British history approaches to learning about minority groups in Britain. A direct approach devoid of an input of knowledge about minority groups quickly lapses into rhetoric; a positive approach that ignores the reality of racism becomes little more than a sentimental celebration of minority cultures. This is true regardless of the age of the pupils being taught. Raising pupils' awareness of racism and increasing their understanding of cultural diversity should be seen as reverse sides of the same coin.

Experiental learning and *the acquisition of facts and skills.* Multicultural education is concerned with increasing pupils' appreciation of their own and others' cultural experience through an informed understanding of the social and historical factors which shape that experience. An undue emphasis on the experiential can mean that pupils never move beyond their own preconceptions and that prejudices are thereby confirmed rather than challenged. To ignore totally the experiential, however, is to run the risk of presenting factual information as inert and intellectual skills as devoid of any personal relevance. A balance needs to be achieved, therefore, between those approaches, such as the direct and to some extent the positive approaches, which have traditionally stressed the experiential dimension of learning, and those which, like the black British and world history approaches, have developed from a strong informational base. Personal growth and intellectual development are both necessary aspects of the urge towards understanding.

Contemporary and *historical perspectives.* Most of the approaches outlined in the previous pages adopt either a contemporary or a historical perspective on racism and cultural diversity. The direct and positive approaches, for example, incline towards a contemporary perspective, while the black British history and the world history approaches are obviously more concerned with past events. Both perspectives are essential. Pupils need to know about causes as well as effects. They need to undersand about the roots of racism as well as about its manifestations in society today; about the patterns of cultural diversity apparent now and the way in which these patterns have developed through history. To some extent this balance can be sought within specific approaches: history is not about a past unrelated to the present, but a past that impinges upon the concerns of the living. The balance can only be fully achieved, however, if pupils are exposed to a range of different approaches.

Local and *global issues.* The patterns of cultural diversity vary enormously from place to place. They are always, however, to some extent shaped by social, economic and historical factors which have a global dimension. The movement of wage labour, which in one context may involve migration across national frontiers, in another may involve little more than a flit from dale to dale. Yet the farm labourer and the migrant worker are participating in a common process. Each is on the move in search of work, wealth, an improved standard of living, or the means of survival. This means that insights culled from both the world history and world studies approaches should be seen in relation to the more local issues stressed by other approaches. Pupils' understanding of cultural diversity within their own locale, or even within Britain as a whole, will be severely limited unless they are able to relate it to what they know of other times and places.

It should be stressed that each of their paired priorities operates at every stage of the child's cognitive development. Pupils do not progress in a linear fashion from an understanding of the local situation to a knowledge of global structures, or from a contemporary to a historical perspective. Nor does an understanding of cultural diversity necessarily have to be achieved before the issue of racism can be tackled in the classroom. On the contrary progression within multicultural education is by means of a constant interaction between varying insights and perspectives. It is spiral rather than linear. The development of a composite strategy is, therefore, as important in the primary as in the secondary school curriculum. Preparing pupils for a multicultural society means enabling them to return time and time again to such key concerns as racial prejudice and discrimination, global in-equality, and the history and cultures of minority groups in Britain.

To sum up. This chapter has outlined certain approaches to multicultural education currently being developed in schools and has related these approaches to the general curriculum aims outlined at the end of chapter 2. None of these approaches is in itself sufficient preparation for life in a multicultural society. Together, however, each complements the others, providing a broad spread of factual information, critical skills, and key concepts. What is needed in schools, therefore, is a composite strategy rather than a reliance on a single approach. Such a strategy, it has been argued, should be operated at every stage of development and awareness. In the following chapter we shall move from a consideration of these general curriculum issues as they affect all pupils to a discussion of the language curriculum of the school as it relates to the special needs of certain minority ethnic group pupils.

CHAPTER SIX

Language Issues

The previous chapters of this book have stressed the relevance of multicultural education to all pupils in all schools regardless of their cultural background or ethnic origin. This chapter takes a narrower focus, concentrating on the special language needs of pupils for whom English is a second language or for whom standard English is sufficiently distinct from their own dialect forms as to require a particular curriculum response. Schools are still learning to recognize these special needs, to acquire the teaching skills necessary to meet them, and to create the organizational structures within which to apply such skills. The following pages point, therefore, to key elements in a pattern of response that is still changing and developing.

PUPILS OF WEST INDIAN ORIGIN

The linguistic situation of pupils of West Indian origin in British schools is highly complex. Since most have been born and brought up in Britain, the influences operating upon their language usage are varied and difficult to classify. Take, for example, the imaginary but not untypical case of a child whose parents speak Barbadian in the home, whose peers speak a version of Jamaican or Cockney in the street, and who is expected to operate in standard English at school. Passage between home, street and school involves such a child in a constant process of what sociolinguists refer to as 'code-switching'.

According to Harold Rosen and Tony Burgess (1980, 35) this code-switching can best be understood in terms of the interaction of two continua. The first of these is the 'Creole continuum'. The language spoken by the vast majority of West Indians in the Caribbean is referred to as 'Creole', 'patois' or 'dialect'. This differs from standard English both in its grammar and in its sound system. However, this differential is not a fixed quantity but operates on a sliding scale according to factors such as the social class of the speaker and the formality of the situation in which the interaction occurs. Each island, moreover, has its own distinct dialect features. This language situation has been described by Viv Edwards as 'a continuum with broad Creole at one end and standard English at the other' (Edwards, 1979, 16).

The language of the West Indian child in the British school system is influenced by a further set of factors. For a second continuum overlays the first. This again has standard English at one end. At the other end of the continuum are local dialect features. These differ from area to area and are never static, acting upon one another to create new dialect formations and linguistic constructions. In London, for example, the Cockney dialect features interact with the predominantly Jamaican patois to produce a distinct variant called 'London/Jamaican'. This, Rosen and Burgess have suggested, 'occupies a unique position for London school pupils' (Rosen and Burgess, 1980, 35).

It also presents teachers with a particular kind of challenge. For traditionally one of the main functions of schooling has been to initiate pupils into the use of standard English. What, then, should be the attitude of teachers to the use of West Indian dialect in the classroom? Should they correct it or condone it? If they correct it, are they damaging the self-identity of the speaker? If, on the other hand, they condone it, are they failing to provide the child with the necessary means of social advancement? These are the kinds of questions that concern teachers and on which there is considerable disagreement within the teaching profession itself and among other interested groups.

Any response to these questions is fraught with problems. On the one hand it is all too easy to stamp on dialects a cultural preservation order that is incomprehensible, if not a cause of resentment, to the dialect users themselves. On the other hand a lack of sensitivity towards the expressive and communicative subtlety of non-standard dialects is equally reprehensible. Following the Bullock Report (Department of Education and Science, 1975, 143), the Rampton Report steered a middle course between these two extreme positions by arguing for a ' "repertoire" approach to the teaching of standard English' (Department of Education and Science, 1981, 72). Such an approach aims at valuing all language and dialects as a vital part of the child's linguistic repertoire. 'The intention', states the Rampton Report, 'is not to change or replace any particular dialect but to develop a sharper awareness of, and interest in, the different language forms that the child can use' (ibid., 24).

As far as developing oral fluency is concerned the repertoire approach has a great deal to commend it. However, there is evidence that in some cases a non-standard spoken dialect can interfere with the pupil's ability to write and read standard English (Edwards, 1979, 62–82). Since the printed language is almost entirely standard this presents a considerable problem. For, without the ability to operate as both reader and writer in standard English, the pupil's capacity to communicate will be severely limited. To accept the notion of 'interference' does not, however, imply a rejection of the repertoire approach. Interference can best be countered, not by a denial of the child's vernacular, but by a clear explanation to the child of how to translate meanings across from the spoken to the written mode. What is needed, therefore, is an understanding by all teachers of the distinction between written and spoken forms and a command of various strategies for making this distinction explicit to the pupils concerned. The changes that are required relate primarily to teachers' awareness, not pupils' speech.

One project which has seriously attempted to build bridges between the spoken and written word is the Reading Through Understanding project based at the ILEA Centre for Urban Education Studies. The purpose of the materials developed by this project was to enable reading to grow out of listening. Thus, one of the units, 'Share-a-Story', suitable for pupils in the 5–11 age range, presents folk stories from Africa and the Caribbean on cassette and in book form. The cassettes can be used by the teacher as a story-telling aid, by pupils in small groups, or by individual pupils. Although designed with pupils of West Indian origin in mind, the materials and the method employed are of value to all early readers (Reading Through Understanding, 1978).

The development of suitable reading materials is an urgent need and one that might well be met by individual schools working through a teachers' centre. This is an area in which parents and the local community should be as fully involved as possible. The Reading Materials for Minority Groups project (1982–5), funded by the All Saints Educational Trust, Middlesex Polytechnic, has been involved in the collection of stories told by parents and members of the local community and the translation of these stories into a variety of non-European languages. These materials (as yet unpublished, but information is available from the Multicultural Study Centre, Middlesex Polytechnic, White Hart Lane, London N17) are intended for use both in the classroom and at home.

Nor should it be forgotten that there is now a well-established tradition of black British literature to which many pupils respond with great interest. Much of this is directly concerned with the experience of being young and black in Britain today and some is written by authors who have been closely involved with the British school sytem. For example, the poet, James Berry (Berry, 1981 and 1982), as the recipient of an Arts Council Writing Fellowship has worked closely with schools, while Donald Hinds, writer and teacher (Hinds, 1966), works full time in the history department of Tulse Hill School in Brixton.

As far as the pupils' own written work is concerned the overriding need is for them to achieve proficiency in standard English, partly because the conventions governing writing are less flexible than those governing speech and partly because there have developed as yet no clear conventions for recording dialect forms in the written word. Clearly, in expressive writing, pupils may need to experiment with written dialect forms. There is, after all, a long tradition of such writing; from Robert Burns through Hugh MacDiarmid to Linton Kwesi Johnson. Transactional or discursive prose requires, however, a command of standard English. Without this the pupil will be severely handicapped. Thus, we can see that as far as the pupil's written work is concerned the stress upon the acquisition of standard English is a top priority. This brings us back to the important notion of 'interference' between spoken dialect and written standard and the kinds of strategies that might be used to counter this effect in the classroom.

There is, it should be admitted, a dilemma here for the serious teacher who has the interests of the pupils at heart. For these interests are not served by denying the pupils' vernacular. Their speech must be valued if their identity is to be affirmed. Yet, if Viv Edwards' findings regarding dialect interference are to be accepted, this affirmation may serve to reinforce some of the problems that the child encounters in learning to read and write. This dilemma can be partly reconciled by means of the repertoire strategy, whereby pupils learn to speak standard English as well as to value their own vernacular. Equally important, however, is to develop in pupils a curiosity about language itself; about how they use it, about the relation between standard and vernacular and between the spoken and written word, and about the conventions governing these forms. Understanding language – its structures, conventions and usage – is an important element in being able to handle it with skill and precision.

ENGLISH AS A SECOND LANGUAGE

If the linguistic challenge facing the child of West Indian origin in British schools involves a complex pattern of code-switching, the challenge to many other minority groups is that of bilingualism. Traditionally, the term 'bilingualism' in this country has been used in connection with European languages. Increasingly, however, the changing population of urban areas demands a reconsideration of this Eurocentric viewpoint. The presence in Britain of Turkish–Cypriot, Moroccan, Punjabi, Bangladeshi and Chinese language communities, to name but a few, has meant that schools have had to redefine what they mean by bilingualism. An estimated 131 languages are now spoken in the area served by the ILEA, 64 in Bradford, 50 in Coventry, and 42 in Peterborough (Linguistic Minorities Project, 1983).

These statistics point to a fine interweaving of language and cultural experience. The following account by a Muslim girl in an east Midlands primary school reveals something of the complexity of this process: 'I speak English at school, Gujerati on my way home to my friends. I read books at the mosque in Urdu and I learn passages from the Koran in Arabic . . . My mum speaks Marathi' (quoted in Houlton, 1983, 6). Linguistic diversity as experienced by this girl, and by many other children in various parts of the country, involves a perpetual crossing and recrossing of social and cultural boundaries.

Broadly speaking this experience of linguistic diversity has two aspects, both of which require urgent and careful consideration: the acquisition by the child of English as a second language and the development of the child's own mother-tongue. These, it should be noted, are two sides of the same coin. Any attempt to extend the expressive and communicative ability of the child must pay due regard to both aspects. The child's mother-tongue is the means by which she gains a sense of herself as a sentient and responsible being, capable of communicating to members of a language community very different from her own and of acquiring the second language necessary to do so.

Nevertheless, mother-tongue teaching and the teaching of English as a second language raise distinct sets of issues, which need to be understood before a coordinated language policy can be developed. As far as English as a second language is concerned, a distinction is often made between 'first' and 'second phase' language needs. In the past it has been assumed that 'first phase' language needs – the needs, that is, of real beginners in English – can be met only if pupils are withdrawn from the ordinary classroom for part, or even all, of the school day. Recently, however, this assumption has been seriously questioned. Josie Levine, for example, has argued against special language classes on the grounds that 'neither the children nor the teachers have access to a wide enough curriculum, socially the children are ghettoised, and the specialist provision (with honourable exceptions) is too much based in the teaching of linguistic structures in isolation from the natural contexts in which they occur' (Levine, 1983, 1).

Instead, Levine has argued, pupils who are learning English as a second language should be taught within the mainstream curriculum by teachers who are responsive to their needs working in partnership with specialist language teachers. Clearly, a mainstreaming strategy of this kind is extremely demanding. It requires, at the very least, flexibility in classroom organization, a wide range of teaching skills, professional collaboration, and an emphasis on collaborative learning among the pupils. Given these conditions, however, it can prove highly effective as a means of enabling pupils to acquire the use of English as a second language through interaction with one another and with curriculum tasks which are both intellectually extending and varied.

Pauline Hoyle, a science specialist who is also a trained

teacher of English as a second language, has given a useful
account of how the mainstreaming strategy can work in
practice:

> Talk is very important in my lessons and I try to get the
> pupils to talk about what they already know before I start
> teaching a topic. For example in the unit on 'Solids,
> Liquids and Gases', the first activity is to classify a whole
> range of objects into those three categories before we've
> even started to talk about properties and definitions. It's
> quite difficult to give them examples of gases that they'll
> know but there's certainly a lot of discussion because
> many of the items fit into two or more categories. This
> sort of discussion gives the second language learners a lot
> of language support because the pupils are focussing on a
> limited range of vocabulary, but such words as 'solid',
> 'liquid' and 'gas' are constantly being repeated, as are
> phrases like: '. . . because it's solid/hard/runny/trans-
> parent, etc.' So by the end of this exploratory exercise
> everyone can pronounce 'solid, liquid and gas', as well as
> a large number of items. In addition they are able to
> justify their own classification. This activity is also very
> valuable for me to assess what prior knowledge the pupils
> have before I do any input. (Hoyle, 1983, 12)

By placing this kind of exploratory talk at the centre of the
educational process, Pauline Hoyle is able to help her pupils
understand scientific concepts and acquire an experimental
attitude towards problems. She is also able to extend significantly the pupils' range of language uses in a variety of written
and spoken forms. For the listening and talking exercises
documented above are reinforced by carefully selected reading
materials and written tasks aimed at increasing the pupils'
mastery of English as a second language.

A common argument against the mainstreaming strategy is
that pupils who have acquired very little English need to be
introduced gradually into the complex language environment
of the school and that a special language unit serves as a useful
transition zone for such pupils. Schools that operate a
withdrawal system of this kind should ensure, however, that as
pupils become increasingly bilingual they lessen their depen-
dence upon the special language unit. The task for the teacher
is to stage this process of integration into the mainstream in

such a way that the pupils are neither socially nor linguistically disadvantaged. These stages, it should be noted, will be linked to developing experience in English rather than to the age of the pupils concerned.

Although schools and local education authorities differ as to how they should organize their response to the 'first phase' language needs of children for whom English is a second language, there is at least, according to the national survey conducted by Alan Little and Richard Willey (1981), a record of continuing provision in this area. Turning to the teaching of English as a second language beyond the initial stages a very different picture emerges:

> There is wide agreement among those responsible for E2L teaching that current provision for the more advanced stages of language work and for teaching specialist subject languages – which are seen as being of crucial importance to academic achievement – is inadequate. There is an urgent need for the development of effective methods of diagnosing needs and monitoring performance, and for meeting more advanced E2L needs across the secondary curriculum. (Little and Willey, 1981, 17)

In highlighting the inadequacy of the resources provided in this area, Little and Willey define the educational problem as a diagnostic one. Teachers, they argue, should be able to recognize those instances where pupils' limited grasp of the English language affects their powers of conceptualization.

This is more difficult than may at first appear. At a certain stage of development second-language learners achieve a degree of fluency which can, as far as the teacher is concerned, mask their continuing special educational needs. For this reason all teachers, regardless of the age range they teach or of their subject specialisms, require information concerning the linguistic background of their pupils. Without this information they will be unable to respond with any degree of sensitivity to the needs of second-language learners in their classrooms. Pupil profiles, documenting the second-language learners' development and offering a cumulative source of information for the pupils themselves, their parents and teachers, are therefore an essential element within the school record system. The purpose of such profiles is to inform teachers' judgements and pupils' self-appraisal, not to provide a means of publicly grading individuals according to their linguistic achievement. These records should, moreover, be seen as the property of the pupils concerned and be handed over to them when they leave school.

In responding to 'second phase' language needs, teachers of pupils for whom English is a second language should also pay particular attention to the social environment of the classroom. Pupils need to be able to talk about their language and learning difficulties without fear of censure or ridicule. This is true of all pupils, but for second-language learners it is particularly important. It is essential, therefore, that the classroom is organized in such a way that the pupils are able to talk to one another as well as to the teacher. Interaction between second-language learners and between these pupils and native English speakers is a vital means of articulating and resolving specific language difficulties relating to the tasks set by the teacher. Every lesson should include at least one opportunity for pupils to share problems and insights with one another.

It follows from this that the use of their mother-tongue by pupils for whom English is a second language is an important aid to learning across the curriculum. Bilingual pupils should be treated as such. Their need to move between languages in communicating with other pupils and discussing the substance of their work in a range of subjects should be respected and catered for. This means that the multiracial classroom should also be a multilingual classroom in which pupils are free to use the full extent of their linguistic competence. Within such a classroom the pupils will, of course, be operating beyond the language capabilities of the teacher. (Unless the teacher happens to be competent in several languages.) This need be no serious drawback, however, provided that the teacher is aware that pupils can learn collaboratively and that, in doing so, they need to utilize all their language resources.

MOTHER-TONGUE TEACHING

The mother-tongue plays a vitally important part in the education and development of all pupils. For native English speakers within the British educational system this need for expressive and communicative interaction within their own language community may present no serious problem. For speakers of Gujerati, however, or Turkish, it presents very serious problems. How can such pupils learn to communicate ideas, to express their own feelings and emotions, to explore relationships across a range of situations, to understand intransigent problems, unless through their first language? The use by pupils of their mother-tongue is the basic requirement of any educational system which aims beyond a mere instrumentalist transmission of skills and facts.

In making this point I am not suggesting that the initiation of non-native English speakers into the use of English is anything other than a top priority. Indeed, the previous section stressed the need for such pupils to acquire competency in both spoken and written English. It should be recognized, however, that in learning English as a second language they are progressing, not towards an exclusive reliance on English, but towards bilingualism. Schools, therefore, should offer an opportunity for interaction between the second language they are acquiring and the first language through which they have already realized some of their expressive and communicative potential.

Critics of this position have argued that arrangements for supporting bilingual pupils' first languages can lead to 'ghettoization' (see, for example, Brookes, 1980). Mother-tongue provision, in other words, can serve to separate pupils from the mainstream of school learning, thereby increasing the likelihood of their continuing underachievement. Within a school system that measures success in terms of the pupil's performance in the mainstream and that culminates at secondary school with its set courses and examination options, this is clearly a serious drawback. Such worries lie at the heart of the seemingly conservative attitude, adopted by many minority-group parents, to mother-tongue teaching in British schools.

This attitude has been fully confronted in a recent statement by Chris Searle on the need for what he calls 'a common language':

Our priority must still be to struggle for mastery of Standard English for *all* our students. Certainly, we must re-create Standard English in the image of its users and its sexist and racist imagery must be exorcised. We also have to re-define our language continually in the process of making a new lexicon that will serve all our children.

Our common language must take on all the muscle, the realism, the figurative and imaginative power to be found in the various mother-tongues of our children, all the strength that has been dammed up and suppressed for generations. (Searle, 1983, 72)

This is a significant statement coming from an educationist and political activist who has previously stressed the power of the vernacular to shape individual and group identity (see, for example, Searle, 1973 and 1975). However, the difference between the earlier and later stance is a matter of emphasis rather than inconsistency. The emergence of a 'common language', as conceived by Searle, relies upon the child's competence both in the mother-tongue and in standard English. Bilingualism – defined in terms of this kind of two-handed competence – remains at the educational cutting edge.

The key question is how schools might be organized in such a way as to support its development. Responses to this might be grouped round three fairly broad strategies:

Reconstructing the notion of 'Modern Languages'. 'Modern Languages' is usually seen in terms of an offering of French, Spanish and, possibly, Italian. Occasionally, Russian teaching is provided as an option for the high-flyers. Rarely is 'Modern Languages', as a curriculum category, defined in terms of the mother-tongue needs of the non-native English speakers attending the school. Indeed, only 4 per cent of the schools in Little and Willey's survey reported any teaching of either Urdu or Punjabi, in spite of the fact that these were the most common Asian languages spoken by pupils (Little and Willey, 1981, 19). Where such teaching does take place it tends to be organized as an extra-curricular activity or as a form of supplementary schooling provided by the minority ethnic groups concerned. If it is ever to find a footing in the mainstream curriculum, it will require a determined effort by local authorities to recruit and, if necessary, train members of minority-language communities to work as language teachers in schools. Then – and only then – might the notion of 'Modern Languages' be reconstructed to meet the mother-tongue needs of pupils for whom English is a second language.

Specialist support within the mainstream curriculum. Specialist language support can also be used to reinforce learning in other subject areas. Viewed as a resource across the mainstream curriculum, the language teacher becomes available to pupils as, and when, needed. The primary task is to enable the pupils to move easily between languages, so that their developing bilingualism becomes a positive asset. In this way a language teacher relates to the ordinary classroom teacher on a collaborative basis, helping pupils to explore through the use of their mother-tongue new concepts, ideas and factual information relevant to the subject-matter being taught and to formulate their own problems and questions which can, then, if necessary, be referred to the subject specialist. Clearly, this strategy is expensive in terms of human resources, which no doubt accounts for why it remains virtually untried. For certain classes in particular schools it may yet prove, however, to be the most effective means of providing specialist mother-tongue support for non-native English speakers.

Informal encouragement of minority languages. Informal encouragement of minority languages within the school can take many forms. In the classroom teachers can actively support the use of these languages by organizing tasks around small group discussions, during which pupils are able to explore together, in their own mother-tongues, new ideas, themes and reading materials. At break, during lunchtime and after school, space can be set aside for pupils to talk together or read quietly. The school bookshop and library can stock a range of books in a variety of languages. Notice boards can display information and posters in the minority languages of the school as well as in English. General signposts around the school and the names of subject departments written on doors can also be presented in a bilingual form. In isolation such gestures might well be written off as tokenism. As accompaniments to genuine curriculum innovation they are valuable means of creating a context for change.

Indeed, small beginnings in this area can prove to be unexpectedly significant in their outcomes. The following account by a teacher of an incident which occurred in the context of the Schools Council Language in the Multicultural Primary Classroom project shows the quality of learning that can result from a skilled, but largely spontaneous, attempt to draw on the linguistic expertise of the pupils themselves:

Well, Lily read me her story, or rather I got her to retell it to me because it was pages and pages long! Anyhow, in this story a little girl falls asleep and wakes up surrounded by African ladies, who say something like, 'Oh la walla walla bim bam' which was Lily's idea of 'African'. Actually, it was much better than that and a very good attempt at inventing a language, as I told her. We talked about 'African'. Lily said she'd never heard 'African' spoken but she did know that Arnold spoke an African language in his home and she thought it was called Ghanaian. I told her that the proper name for his home language was Twi and would she like to ask Arnold how to say whatever it was. What were the ladies saying, anyhow? Lily said they were saying, 'Who is this little girl?' So we asked Arnold but it was too sophisticated a problem for him – he speaks Twi at home and English at school but he can't switch from one to the other at will yet. I suggested we went to Pierre, Arnold's big brother, but before we went off to the third year class to find him, we talked around the incident in the story a bit more. I reversed the situation and asked Lily – if it had been a little African girl who woke up surrounded by English ladies, how she thought English would have sounded to her? She found that difficult. I don't blame her. I suggested it might sound quite strange – perhaps something like – 'Oh oo la la pooh pooh!' It was silly but it made her laugh. Then I asked her if she would mind if people thought that English sounded like that – would she feel upset? She thought about it and said she might. At this point we went off to find Pierre and hear what real 'African' or Twi sounded like. Pierre was just writing out his Viking story but he was very patient and helpful. Not only was he able to translate but he told us some very interesting things about Twi word order and patiently coached Lily's pronunciation. He couldn't write the sentence but he's going to ask his mum for that and teach Lily later. Lily's really chuffed with herself now that she can speak a sentence in Twi. (Language in the Multicultural Primary Classroom, 1982)

This incident occurred in a second-year junior classroom. Because of the teacher's willingness to recognise the classroom as multilingual as well as multicultural, Lily was able to learn something about her own and others' attitudes towards language and, more specifically, about how word order in Twi differs from that in English. The incident also showed that teachers are learners too. It was Pierre who provided the necessary expertise and skills and who made these available both to Lily and to the teacher. The value placed in this situation on the competence of non-native English speakers with regard to their own native languages lies at the heart of effective mother-tongue teaching.

Many of the points made in this and the previous section with regard to bilingualism are highlighted by John Wright in the six criteria which he has presented as a means of evaluating work in multiracial schools:

One: Bring minority languages into the learning situation for utilitarian, not tokenist reasons.

Two: Integrate the work stimulated by minority language books/tapes/workcards etc with the mainstream of class activity.

Three: Provide within the classroom the opportunity of developing and refining the skills of bilingualism – translation and interpretation – not only of language but of cultural experience.

Four: Provide language learning opportunities, and the opportunity of becoming bilingual, to all students – even though a very small minority of English speaking students would take up the option.

Five: Never segregate the minority group for mother-tongue learning. Always explicitly invite *all* pupils/students to join the group, even if only a few will.

Six: Preserve and defend the minority group students' rights to choose for her/himself the balance of minority and majority group language and culture which best meets the desired identity of the individual. (Wright, 1982, 19–20)

These criteria, it should be noted, relate to the work of all teachers, not just those who hold special language posts. If non-native English speakers are present in a group the teacher ought to be aware of this and ought to utilize the expertise within the group to enhance the learning of all.

LANGUAGE AWARENESS

There is now a fairly well-established tradition in schools of studying language as it is actually used rather than as an abstract system of grammatical rules and syntactical structures. The publication in 1971 of an influential handbook for teachers entitled *Language in Use* (Doughty et al., 1971) did a great deal to further the development of this tradition. In 1974 it was given an increased impetus with the publication of the first issue of what was intended to be a series of occasional reports from the Language and Class Workshop based at the University of London Institute of Education (Language and Class Workshop, 1974). These reports, containing transcriptions of the recorded speech of young people and adults, showed how valuable documents of this kind can be as a classroom resource. Although the thrust of the Language and Class Workshop papers, with their stress on working-class speech, was very different from that of the *Language in Use* materials, both highlighted the need for teachers and pupils to study language as it is used in the street, at home, at work and at school. As such, they served to redefine the parameters of the language curriculum operating at both the primary and secondary levels.

This shift towards a study of the everyday functions of language has particular implications for the teacher working in a multilingual or multidialectal context. For the ability to switch from one language to another or one dialect to another requires a keen sense of the diversity of language use and of the social conventions that govern the selection and operation of different linguistic forms. Pupils require particular help in this area. They need information concerning the range of language diversity within contemporary Britain, opportunities for exploring their own and others' attitudes towards minority languages, and practice in using language within a variety of situations. Enabling pupils to understand language in its diversity of usage should be an important aspect of the language curriculum of any school. Within the multiracial school it is an indispensable element. Without some such understanding no learning of any kind is possible.

Information about diversity. Towards the end of their investigation into the language of London school children Rosen and

Burgess noted 'that linguistic diversity was, if handled imaginatively, a potentially rich curriculum resource, and that language diversity of all kinds could be the core of language study' (Rosen and Burgess, 1980, 119). The kind of evidence collected in that investigation might, in other words, itself be an important source of information for pupils as well as teachers. Seen in this light the study of language is much more than any mere training in language skills. Language is to be understood in its full diversity as well as used. Indeed, unless it is understood in this way, it cannot be used with any degree of skill or sensitivity. The suggestion here, then, is that the appraisal of language should be extended to cover as broad a range of usage as possible (the pupils' own speech, for example, their parents', other adults') and that materials illustrative of this range should be developed as an essential element within the language curriculum.

Attitudes to language. Such appraisal necessarily involves an examination by the pupils of attitudes towards their own speech and that of others. The notions of 'correctness' and 'appropriateness' need to be discussed as conflicting criteria for judging language usage. Various linguistic conventions also need exploring in this context together with the implications of maintaining or breaking these conventions. The stress throughout should be on the value of non-standard English and non-native languages. The aim of such work would be to increase the pupils' appreciation of language in its diversity and to encourage them to use language imaginatively across the full range of their repertoire. At the same time the importance of standard English as a means of access to power and status within British society would be recognized and discussed with pupils as an issue in its own right. The value of an ongoing dialogue with pupils about their own relationship with language cannot be overestimated.

Language in practice. In order to extend their own range of language uses pupils need to be able to experiment with language in a variety of situations. Role-play and improvised drama can serve as useful teaching aids in this respect. By adopting roles within a fictional situation pupils are able to make linguistic demands upon themselves without having to suffer the consequences of failing to meet these demands. The problem, for example, of how to contradict someone who is in a position of authority over one, which in real life might well lead to anxiety or embarrassment, becomes within the context of the drama an opportunity for increased insight into how language operates in practice. Drama can thus be a way of holding complex situations in frame so as to analyse and replay them at will. Beyond specific drama activities of this kind it is also important that pupils are given the opportunity to interact in as wide a range of social situations as possible (in pairs, small groups, addressing a large group, talking with adult visitors) and to reflect upon these at their own pace.

These three elements within the language curriculum require careful consideration by all teachers regardless of their subject specialism. If our pupils are to forge for themselves a language that is at once richly expressive and powerfully communicative, they will need to hammer it out on the subject-matter of the whole curriculum. This means that all teachers must see their professional concerns as fronting onto the task of language development. They must ensure that their pupils are able to operate across the full range of their linguistic repertoire and that they are able to distinguish the substance of an argument from the form in which it is couched. An effective language curriculum enables all pupils to revel in their own and others' linguistic expertise while developing an increasingly discriminating sense of judgement concerning the views and opinions expressed. The study of language involves both practice and appraisal.

To sum up. This chapter has attempted to show the complexity of the linguistic situations in which many pupils are placed. In responding to this complexity it is essential that schools actively encourage pupils, in all subjects and at all ages, to develop their expertise across the full range of their linguistic ability, from standard English to their own vernacular. This means, in practical terms, the development of a repertoire strategy for dialect users and, for speakers of minority languages, the coordination of a full bilingual programme, incorporating the teaching of English as a second language and mother-tongue teaching in the main minority languages represented within the school. These strands should be seen as part of a whole-school language policy which places linguistic diversity at the centre of its concerns, both in terms of the skills to be developed and in terms of the pupils' knowledge of the range of languages and dialects spoken in contemporary English. The language environment of the school is not self-contained. It is part of a much broader communicative framework which encompasses the home and the local community. The problem of how to forge stronger links between the various elements within this framework is the subject of the following chapter.

CHAPTER SEVEN

Parents and the Community

In 1977 the Taylor Report stated: 'It is the individual parent who is in law responsible for securing his child's education and whose support in this task is vital. There should therefore be at the individual level also a partnership between home and school' (Department of Education and Science, 1977, 43). Since the publication of that report, the idea of 'a partnership between home and school' has been the subject of political debate, legislative action and professional concern. In each of these spheres discussion has centred on three main issues: the constitution of the governing body of the school, the right of choice for parents about which school to send their child, and their right of access to information held by the school on that child. Each of these issues has been sharpened by the frequently expressed sense of alienation felt by working-class and black parents in relation to the British school system. This chapter looks at some of the ways in which schools might begin to redefine their role within the community so as to bridge what, according to the Rampton Report, has become a 'wide gulf in trust and understanding' (Department of Education and Science, 1981, 41).

LEGISLATION IS NOT ENOUGH

Hard on the heels of the Taylor Report the Conservative Party 1979 Election Manifesto promised to give parents greater influence over education by granting them the right of choice between schools. Referring to its proposals as 'our parents' charter', the Conservative Party resolved to 'place a clear duty on government and local authorities to take account of parents' wishes when allocating children to schools' (Conservative Party, 1979, 291–2). Accordingly, on coming to power it proposed an education bill which was passed by Parliament a year later.

The Education Act 1980 does not in fact give parents the right of choice between schools. Instead, it grants them the right 'to express a preference . . . and to give reasons for this preference' (Section 6 (1)). Even this minimal right is whittled away by the right of the local education authority to ignore the preference stated 'if compliance with the preference would prejudice the provision of efficient education or the efficient use of resources' (Section 6 (3) (a)). Although local education authorities are, under the terms of the act, obliged to set up appeals procedures against admission decisions (Section 7), the legal rights of parents as defined in the act fall far short of those promised in 'our parents' charter' of the previous year.

In tracing this history I am not trying to score a party political point, but to stress that legislation is not enough. The weakness of legislation in this area becomes even more apparent if we turn to the question of school government. According to Section 2 of the Education Act 1980, school governing bodies must now include a parent or parents elected by the whole parent body. For those who would wish to see a greater representation of black and working-class parents on school governing bodies, this ruling poses a number of problems. These were articulated clearly in a recent interview with Ambrozine Neil of the Association for Educational Advance:

I think that part of the law has literally no significance. I'll tell you why. There are two reasons.

First, headmasters and headmistresses are tin gods. And they are extremely intelligent people. They know what they want and they are able to assess which parents will 'fit in' and which parents will cause trouble for them. They inform the parents they want to be governors. They tell them it is a good idea to stand for election. When these elections happen at the PTA's, the people at the PTA's get the idea which parent the head wants to see elected.

The other reason is that every parent cares first of all about their own child or children. To stand for election as a parent governor, you have to have a child at the school. If something is wrong at the school parent-governors will want to speak up for all children. But this might mean going against the head and maybe teacher representatives on the governors. Because they must worry about their own child, they are sometimes afraid of the possibility of a backlash against their own child in the school. This makes it a difficult position to be in. (Neil, 1982, 6)

Some readers may find this hard to swallow. Yet the points Ambrozine Neil makes are fundamental to any attempt to forge closer links between the school and the community. For she reminds us that the notion of a 'parent body' is a misleading metaphor. Parents share in the divisions between the social classes and ethnic groups from which they derive. Communities are in the main fractured and deeply fissured by social inequality. The idea of election by the whole parent body is, therefore, erroneous. Black and working-class families are likely to fall foul of this romanticized view of a unified community. A ruling is required whereby the place of such parents on governing bodies is guaranteed in those schools that serve their needs.

This was, presumably, the point being made by the Rampton Report when it suggested that 'one way in which West Indian parents can be actively involved in shaping the school's overall policies including its curriculum is through appointment to school governing bodies' (Department of Education and Science, 1981, 44). Unfortunately, however, the actual recommendation made by Rampton on this point is somewhat ambiguous or, at least, open to interpretation, since it simply charges local education authorities with the responsibility for ensuring that 'ethnic minority interests are fully taken into account' in the appointment of school governors (ibid., 46). There is no stipulation here, it should be noted, concerning the composition of the governing body. Nevertheless, the spirit, if not the letter, of Rampton is, I think, clear: the governing bodies of multiracial schools should include members of minority ethnic groups.

Given that in most areas this must remain a very distant goal, a number of practical suggestions made by the Afro-Caribbean Education Resource Project in its comments on the

Rampton Report are particularly helpful. These include the recommendation that 'schools should devise ways of ensuring that parents know each other before electing the parent governors' and 'should actively encourage parent governors to meet with parents, to report on their work and to discuss matters of concern with parents' (Afro-Caribbean Education Resource Project, undated, 4.5a and b). The school might also encourage closer liaison and consultation between parents and the community representatives on the governing body. Indeed, Ambrozine Neil's reservations concerning the power of parent governors to effect change within the school would suggest that the role of the community representatives is crucial in any effective representation of minority groups. Procedures such as these, if implemented, would go some way towards compensating for the inadequacies of existing legislation and thereby creating a more democratic system of school government.

If teachers rely solely upon the 1980 Education Act to create community links for them, then schools will become increasingly isolated and will continue to alienate many of the parents and pupils they purport to serve. Legislation, it must be repeated, is not enough. Indeed, it barely begins to address the urgent question of how to share decision-making power and create a curriculum that might reflect more truthfully the concerns and needs felt by minority groups. It is to innovative and socially committed teachers that we must look for an articulate response to this question.

THE OPEN SCHOOL

Teachers, in short, must learn to listen. This is not easy for any group of professionals, but for those whose authority is far too often vested in their capacity to talk at length on a variety of subjects it is an extremely difficult task. The willingness of teachers to expose themselves to face-to-face interaction with parents and to give them open access to school records pertaining to the achievement and progress of individual pupils is crucial in this respect. The mark of extended professionalism must be seen as a willingness to move beyond the limits of one's own expertise and to identify with the problems and dilemmas of the parents and pupils for whose benefit the school exists. In making this movement many teachers may feel out of their depth. They may even feel incompetent. Unless they are willing to put themselves at risk in this way, however, there can be little hope of placing the school at the service of the whole community.

Face-to-face contact

Ironically, the very mechanisms by which schools try to involve parents may serve to increase their sense of alienation. Here, for example, is a black parent talking about the importance of parental involvement in schools:

> Concerning Parent Teacher Groups and meetings – it depends on what the group is like. Some groups actually discuss the children and their problems. Other groups tend to concentrate on raising funds to buy curtains and nonsense like that. But I think it's important to discuss the children and how they're getting on because that's the whole point of it. And therefore if your school is one where you're discussing your children's future, then I think it's fine, but otherwise it's a waste of time. (AFFOR, 1982, 38)

This parent is very clear about what it is she wants from her involvement with the school. She wants to be able to talk with her child's teachers about the education of her child. She is also, however, very clear about what she does not require from the school. She is not looking to the school as a means of extending her social life and mentions the cosiness of certain parent–teacher groups as being a barrier to the development of genuine dialogue between parents and teachers. Equally, she might have mentioned the strained formality of many parents' evenings, with their lack of privacy or of any opportunity for sustained consultation. Or she might have pointed to the difficulty parents sometimes have in making contact, not with the head of year or head of house, nor with the head of department or even the head of school, but with those teachers who actually teach their children. The bureaucracy of the school – however caring and well intentioned are those who operate it – can act as a block to important face-to-face exchanges between parents and teachers.

The first step towards creating a more open school must, therefore, be a thorough review of the procedures governing parental and community access. Rather than adding to these procedures, or instituting new ones, it might be more effective to begin stripping away the old ones. The procedures relating to the employment of non-certified teachers and to the involvement of parents and ancillary workers in the classroom are a case in point. In the present economic climate there is justifiable resistance, by those who take the view that unemployed teachers should have priority when work is being handed out or discussed, to any attempt at challenging existing practice in this area. There is, nevertheless, a need for a much wider definition of who can be involved in the teaching role, so that, for example, many of the community language speakers already concerned with the school – school keepers, nursery nurses, dinner persons, parents, governors – can also be involved in the academic and pastoral curricula. Opening up the teaching role in this way is, of course, also a way of opening up the possibility of a much broader-based public resistance to central and local government policies that lead to teacher unemployment. Parents working alongside teachers are much more likely to see the inanity of teacher unemployment.

A second step is to ensure that the school is always welcoming, that there is always at least one interview room for use by staff and parents, and that if parents are to be kept waiting they should be told why and how long they might be expected to wait. These points may sound obvious, but in the majority of cases they are overlooked: schools are not geared to informal or 'crisis' visits by parents, and teachers lower in status than a pastoral or year head are likely to be faced with the embarrassing situation of having to conduct an interview with parents in the corridor. The parents understandably feel affronted. The real fault, however, lies in the funding priorities of those who control the purse strings. Teachers, even in the most sympathetic local education authorities, have been harassed by school amalgamations and closures and by threats of redeployment and redundancy. This makes it extremely difficult for them to extend their professional role in any way. Central and local government must take the lead if schools are to serve the community.

Thirdly, schools should think carefully about the venue and timing of meetings between parents and teachers. More often than not the school will be the most convenient place for parents and teachers to meet. In certain instances, however, the physical location of various activities (e.g. pastoral work and information sessions) could be shifted to, say, a local community centre or church hall. An ideal site for discussions between parents and teachers is the home. Given the present pressure on teachers, the idea of extending the pastoral role from school to home in this way remains utopian. Nevertheless, among some groups of highly committed teachers home visiting is an important aspect of the pastoral support offered by the school. The appointment of community liaison coordinators, although important in itself, cannot compensate for the lack of dialogue between parents and teachers. Indeed, if an appointment of this kind is seen as a substitute for such dialogue, rather than as a means of facilitating it, it will only serve to erect yet another bureaucratic barrier to effective face-to-face contact.

Freedom of information

If the debate about education in and for a multicultural society is to be broadened to include a wider range of parental opinion, it is essential that parents have access, not only to the teachers of their children, but also to any information held by the school on these children. This is an emotive issue and one to which teachers frequently respond by appealing to the notion of professional privilege. Teachers, it is claimed, need to pass on to one another frankly and without fear of recrimination, important information about their pupils and can only do so provided that record cards remain closed to both parents and pupils. In contrast to this claim a growing number of parents, pupils and teachers take the view that access to such records should be open. The report of a conference organized jointly by Haringey Black Pressure Group on Education and Haringey National Association for Multiracial Education states this position unequivocally: 'school record cards should be open and schools should publicise the fact that records/reports are open to the parents at any time' (Black Pressure Group on Education, 1984).

This recommendation had in fact been made equally strongly seven years earlier in a 'note of extension' to the Taylor Report. Seven members of the committee added their names to this 'note of extension' which suggested 'that it is not enough that individual parent's access to information should be expressed as a "reasonable expectation". It should be a right'. They went on to specify the parent's right of access to 'records kept in a permanent form in the school' as an instance of the general right of all parents to have access to any information concerning the education of their children (Department of Education and Science, 1977, 121). Not surprisingly, since this argument was not even included in the main body of the Taylor Report, the Education Act of 1980 made no mention of any such right. Section 8 of the act, which deals with the question of information from schools to parents, is couched in terms of the responsibilities of local education authorities rather than the rights of parents and is limited in its terms of reference to information concerning admission arrangements.

The Rampton Report, in its recommendations on this issue, offers no radical alternative to the perspective adopted in the legislation of the previous year. Welcoming the provisions in the act requiring local education authorities to publish annually detailed information about their schools, it simply recommends that this information should be 'easily understood by parents, particularly those from ethnic minority groups, and by the wider community' (Department of Education and Science, 1981, 46). While stressing the importance of regular, accurate and detailed school reports and of active parent–teacher associations, it does not affirm parental right of access to information contained in school records. According to the report it is the school that should decide what information is given to the parents and not the parents themselves. Among many individual black parents and black parent pressure groups this remains a major weakness of the Rampton Report and a rallying point for future action.

If the notion of 'a partnership between home and school' as couched in the Taylor Report is to be anything other than empty rhetoric, schools must give parents all the means necessary to play their part in the education of their children. These means, as we have seen, include access to serious educational discussion with the teachers concerned and, as I am now suggesting, access to all information upon which teachers make their judgements and formulate their expectations of individual pupils. Without this access education will remain a purely 'professional' concern from which very many parents will continue to feel alienated. Clearly, in recognizing the right of parents to consult their children's files, the school will need to assume responsibility for deciding exactly what kinds of information should be recorded. An assessment of the pupil's achievement in each subject area together with evidence to support this assessment should form the basis of the record. In the case of information concerning serious breaches of discipline a statement by the pupil should be included if that pupil so wishes.

Unless accompanied by a genuine desire among all teachers to create closer links between home and school, granting parents access to pupil files will accomplish very little. Teachers need to work on many fronts if they are to help produce a more open system of schooling. The following checklist of questions produced by Brent local education authority serves as a useful summary of issues that schools might consider in attempting to involve parents more fully in the education of their children:

- Is the use of jargon in letters to parents avoided?
- Are letters written in languages which are the most appropriate to parents?
- Is the strategy of parents' evening suited to the parents or do the parents have to fit into 'the system'?
- Is the strategy of parents' evening really designed to cater for one hundred per cent attendance by parents?
- Is non-attendance of parents at formal parents' evening interpreted as lack of interest in the child's education?
- Is the suitability of the strategy in operation ever questioned and are other strategies considered?
- Are parents only seen when problems occur?
- Are teachers encouraged to meet parents in routine non-problem situations?
- Is this achieved by home visiting or by holding routine clinics in school?
- Are teachers aware of parents with particular expertise and knowledge who may be able to contribute to the resources of the school?
- Are suitably qualified parents utilized in any way as a non-teaching resource? (Brent London Borough, 1983, 23–4)

THE SCHOOL WITH THE COMMUNITY

These questions remind us, by implication, that parents are a wide, disparate group and that there is always a danger of the parental links forged by the school extending only to a small coterie. This rather obvious point is overlooked in the recent government Green Paper, *Parental Influence at School* (Department of Education and Science, 1984a), in which school accountability is discussed only in terms of ensuring a majority of parents on governing bodies. Any such legislative initiative as that recommended in the Green Paper would in fact barely begin to address the problem of how schools might communicate across the boundaries of class, race and culture. For the popular mandate of the parent governor is often extremely limited. If the school is to address the needs of all the families it serves, it must reach out to the disparate community of which each family is a part.

Legislation on its own, to return to the main theme of this chapter, is not likely to give parents any real power to influence school decision-making. For parents to want to win and exercise such power, schools have to demonstrate that education is important. Schools can best do this by reaching out to parents on issues that concern the local community. The school thus becomes an outward-looking institution – a campaigning institution even – which draws up its agenda of concerns and its programme of action as much from dialogue with the community as from its own professional preoccupations. Teachers in such a school achieve professional identity, not through working *for* the community, but by working in partnership *with* it.

At a time when teachers are frequently accused of encroaching upon the territory of the social worker and the therapist, the idea of the school working with the community is an important means of redefining the role of the teacher as primarily an educational one. For what brings schools and communities into genuine partnership is a shared commitment to education. It is those schools that set themselves apart from the concerns of the local community that are most likely to define their relationship to it in terms of some kind of compensation for social and psychological disadvantage. In working alongside parents and community organizations on issues which concern them, teachers can only serve to reaffirm the central importance of education in the lives of all their pupils.

The following account by a primary school teacher of the Fulham 'Save Our Baths Campaign' shows how just such an issue can be brought into school and taken out again as part of a community campaign while still providing a valuable educational experience:

> The Fulham Baths issue occurred in our locality and was of great importance to the children. The Council decided to close the Baths, which included swimming pool, laundry and slipper baths, claiming that the structure was dangerous. Opponents claimed that this was an excuse, a small expenditure would make the baths safe, and that the site was earmarked for development. Immediate savings and lucrative development prospects in the future were claimed as the real reason for closure. There was a big campaign in which many children took part when they realised that their leisure time and school swimming was at risk. We discussed the issue at school, basing it on evidence from local newspapers and the broadsheet produced by the SOB (Save Our Baths) Campaign. We did some role play in which pensioners and children took on a cost cutting councillor. We spent an art lesson making Save Our Baths posters, and a language lesson writing open letters to the Council arguing the case for saving the baths. We discussed how these could usefully be used and decided to take them down to the baths for the workers to use. They were displayed outside the building when the baths were eventually occupied by local people . . .
>
> One wonders how many opportunities of this kind are being missed by teachers, when so much is happening in many towns and cities which affects the lives of local communities. For example, the closure of factories. A factory closure may not touch the immediate lives of children in the same way as a swimming pool, though it may be ultimately more devastating if their parents work there, and will certainly affect the community as a whole. Should not young people learn to understand the forces at work around them? (Issues in Race and Education, 1982, 14)

Another teacher tells how, by organizing a meeting for parents and other members of the local community about the implications of the Nationality Act, she inadvertently provided an ideal opportunity for serious discussion between parents and teachers on educational matters:

After the talk, there were several questions, based on individual anxieties and people sat around waiting for a chance to discuss their own particular case with the speaker from the Law Centre. While they were waiting many of the parents began to question closely the teachers who had come along about the books on the shelves in the library, about the way in which we taught their children, and about the progress of their own children and particular areas of concern. That wasn't what they had come to talk about, but maybe that's why the talk about their children was much more relaxed and open than any of us teachers present could remember from previous open evenings, and other formal occasions set up for the purpose of discussing 'educational matters'. Another positive factor may have been that the teachers present at the meeting, simply by being there, were openly demonstrating concern for the effects of our immigration and nationality laws on black families – showing solidarity. (ibid., 11)

These two cases stand as examples of how parental demands and community issues can and should be translated into good practice at both the classroom and school level. Clearly, the relevance of particular issues will vary from community to community. In one area it may be the threat of a school closure that will focus community action; in another it may be the continuing underachievement of a particular group of pupils. The important point is that teachers should respond promptly to the concerns of the community and should work alongside parents and community organizations in alleviating the causes of those concerns. There are, nevertheless, two important issues of general concern which are consistently overlooked by schools and ignored by local education authorities in their policy documents and deliberations. Both these issues strike to the heart of the deep social divisions within British society and urgently require a joint response by the school and those sections of society that suffer as a result of those divisions.

Police, schools and the community

The relationship between a school and the local police force is one of the most critical topics to have emerged in the 1980s.

Yet very few schools have a clearly formulated policy to cover the various aspects of this relationship and even less have a policy which results from joint discussions between the police, the school and the community. The result of this unwillingness to confront the issue can be as disastrous as that recorded in the following account taken from evidence given to the Scarman Inquiry and cited by Kathryn Riley:

> M, a black former pupil, revisits the school to keep an appointment with a member of staff. A senior teacher, who is new to the school and therefore unaware that he is talking to a former pupil, calls the police because, as he puts it later, the boy did not show 'due deference'. When the police arrived, M was in the school tuck shop in the company of the member of staff with whom he had the appointment. He was pulled out of the shop and pinned to the ground by several policemen. At one point there were thirteen policemen in the school playground. This all took place in front of young impressionable pupils waiting to buy goods from the tuck shop. (Riley, 1982, 3)

This incident occurred in Brixton in February 1981, a month before what Lord Scarman was later to refer to as 'the Brixton disorders'.

It is not enough to suggest, as Scarman does, that greater police involvement in schools – through participation in discussion groups, classes on the police, and road safety activities – will resolve the problem and to express the 'hope that teachers and parents will welcome and encourage this' (Scarman, 1982, 166). Black pupils and their parents do not need the Policy Studies Institute, whose report, *Police and People in London*, is undoubtedly the most detailed and extensive study to date of contemporary British policing, to inform them that 'the level of racial prejudice in the Force is cause for concern' (Policy Studies Institute, 1983, 4, 351). They know it from their own experience. It is highly unlikely, therefore, that attempts to increase police involvement in schools will be welcomed by the black community, unless these attempts are accompanied by a frank recognition of racism within the police force together with serious and widespread discussion concerning the implications of that racism and the need for greater community control of the police.

This point is acknowledged by the Policy Studies Institute,

which in the recommendations to its report stresses the need
for 'explicit discussion and thinking about the ethnic dimension
in policing' and, in particular, the 'need to expose police
officers to the views and attitudes of people outside the Force,
especially members of ethnic minority groups' (ibid., 4, 351).
At the school level such discussion might usefully include a
consideration of the following questions:

- Under what circumstances should the police be called
  into the school?
- What steps should be taken to ensure that, if and when
  the police are called in, their presence causes the least
  possible disturbance?
- What are the responsibilities of the school with regard to
  any pupil taken into police custody?
- Ought the police ever to be invited to participate in
  classroom activities? If so, what procedures should be
  adopted to ensure that this is an educative and informative
  experience?

Open discussion of these issues by the police, the school and
the community is not, of course, a guarantee of progress. It is,
however, a necessary condition. Without a willingness to enter
into genuine dialogue with teachers, parents and members of
the local community, the police force cannot hope to participate
in any useful way in the life of the school.

The questions raised above are sensitive ones and require
careful handling. Teachers, whether they like it or not, are
themselves agents of social control and cannot afford to enter
the debate in a spirit of self-righteousness. Equally, though, the
police cannot afford to adopt a defensive position. The warning
given by Paul Boateng is as relevant to local discussions
concerning the role of the police in schools as it is to the
national debate on police accountability:

We must not conduct this debate on the basis that those
who call for reform of our existing institutions are
somehow subversive. It seems that anyone who calls for
radical changes in the institutions and methods of
policing is labelled 'anti-police' and regarded as someone
who desires to let loose elements whose main aim is to
bring about the end of law and order and civilised
behaviour as we know it. This is a dangeorus myth . . . we

all have a common interest in maintaining the position in which our institutions are capable of changing and altering and adapting to a society that is very different from the one which existed when they were instituted. We have to recognise that the debate must be couched in these terms, and not in the terms of polarisation that it sometimes is. (Boateng, 1984, 158–9)

School and after

A second important issue requiring urgent action by school and community relates to the kinds of support that should be offered to pupils after they have left school. Teachers can hardly claim to be 'in loco parentis' unless they take seriously their continuing responsibility for young people whom they have taught. This is particularly so in an age of widespread unemployment when many of the pupils we teach are destined for the dole queue. Even those who gain employment may benefit from a continuing relationship with the school they attended and those who taught them.

In making this point I am not underestimating the importance of a fully structured careers education programme running throughout the school and supported by a full-time trained careers teacher. On the contrary, such a programme is essential and should be an integral part of every pupil's social and pastoral curriculum. While no pupil should be educated for unemployment, all pupils should be informed about the reality of unemployment in contemporary society and about their rights as unemployed persons. This much is spelled out clearly in the recommendations of the Rampton Report (Department of Education and Science, 1981, 59) and is now being implemented, with varying degrees of success, by schools up and down the country. The kinds of questions that schools might consider when developing a careers programme have been usefully summed up in a checklist produced by the ILEA:

  – Is the advice of teachers – both subject specialists and those concerned with the pastoral care of pupils – linked to the broad careers support within the school to provide effective help and guidance for the individual pupil?
  – Does the school offer careers counselling facilities

which are effective in meeting the needs of pupils from all ethnic groups?

- What does the school do to counter any stereotyping of pupils on racial or cultural grounds which may adversely affect their choice of careers?
- Does the school help pupils to understand the potential opportunities of a wider range of occupations than those open to their parents or grandparents, who first settled in this country?
- Does the school have a strategy for meeting the career needs of pupils who enter school from overseas in the later years of secondary school?
- Does the school observe and monitor the experience of pupils from all ethnic groups when they transfer from school to further or higher education, training, work or unemployment? (Inner London Education Authority, 1981, 16)

That last question points to an area of serious neglect within contemporary schooling. Teachers in fact know very little about what happens to those they have taught. Monitoring the experience of school-leavers would enable teachers to perceive recurring patterns and locate the special needs of particular groups. For example, the Rampton Report suggested that entry to apprenticeship schemes was, in the main, limited to those with close family connections and that young people of West Indian origin were, therefore, often unfairly excluded from such training programmes (Department of Education and Science, 1981, 153–4). If this is still the case, then teachers need to be aware of it. They also need to know whether the effects of this discrimination are limited to those of West Indian origin or whether, as seems likely, it also operates against other groups of migrant workers and their families. By collecting information of this kind schools could begin to act more effectively on behalf of their former pupils, by offering them some kind of counsultancy service on matters relating to education and employment and by initiating discussions with local employers and institutions of further and higher education concerning the needs of the community and how these might best be met. The school's relationship to the school-lever should be one of ongoing commitment.

SUPPLEMENTARY SCHOOLS

In looking at the ways in which schools might begin to redefine their role within the community, teachers can learn a great deal from the development of supplementary education over the last ten years. Supplementary schools, or Saturday schools as they are sometimes called, are, like the Sunday school movement of the last century, a direct response to the failure of the state to provide adequately for the educational needs of particular groups of children. Precisely because they point so accurately to weaknesses in the existing school system, supplementary schools should be assisted financially by local education authorities and viewed as equal partners by those working in mainstream schools.

The West Indian supplementary school movement has been well documented by Maureen Stone (1981), who has highlighted its very real achievements in providing large numbers of black British children with a means of improving their academic work. Less well documented are those supplementary schools that provide instruction in the religion of a particular religious group or offer to children of minority groups lessons in their mother-tongue. These groups include Europeans (Italians, Poles, Cyriots and Spanish) and Asians (Bengali, Hindu and Urdu speakers). Very often, particularly among the Asian communities in Britain, one supplementary school will include religious and cultural subjects in its curriculum as well as language tuition.

J. S. Nagra, in his survey of Asian supplementary schools in Coventry, defines the aims of these schools as follows:

1. To enable the children to communicate with their parents and other persons of their own community;
2. To give the children a clear sense of identity;
3. To assist them to understand and hence participate more fully in their particular social and cultural environment;
4. To pass on religion and culture. (Nagra, 1981, 431)

Given that these are nine such schools in Coventry, catering for 1,500 young people and organized entirely by the communities themselves, there can be no doubting the genuine need for supplementary education of this kind.

The Islamic Studies School in Coventry serves as a useful example of Asian supplementary schooling. Run by the Hillfields Gujerati Muslim Society, this school was opened in 1976 and runs weekday and evening classes for 50 students between the ages of five and fourteen. Although the main aim of the school is religious education, it also offers tuition in Urdu. Boys and girls are taught separately by teachers who give their service voluntarily. The West Indian supplementary school curriculum tends to be broader (see figure 3) and aims at building upon the structure of subjects offered within the mainstream school. While the emphasis is on the acquisition of 'basic' skills, the timetable leaves room for a varied curriculum input and gives most pupils the opportunity of working with those younger and older than themselves during at least some of the sessions. A timetable in fact gives little impression of the diversity of experience avi.lable within supplementary education schemes. There are, as Maureen Stone has pointed out, 'many outings and activities associated with the Saturday

		6.45–7.30 pm	7.50–8.30 pm	
Monday	Junior	Mathematics	Mathematics	
	Senior	Mathematics	Mathematics	
Tuesday	Mixed	Physics	Physics	
Wednesday	Junior	Basic Maths	Basic English	
	Senior	Chemistry	Chemistry	
Thursday	Mixed	Introductory Zoology	Introductory Botany and Rural Science	

N.B.   During the weeknight sessions assembly is held between 6.30 and 6.45 pm and breaktime between 7.30 and 7.50 pm

		10.15–11.00 am	11.00–35 am	12.15–1.00 pm
Saturday	Junior	Basic Maths	Written English	Introductory Science
	Senior	Oral English	Written English	Mathematics

N.B.   On the Saturday assembly is held between 10.00 and 10.15 am and refreshments and games between 11.35 and 12.15 pm

Figure 3 *Timetable for the Paddington Supplementary Education Scheme 1981–2*
Source: Cleveland, 1983, 109.

schools which make them part of the family's life' and help create an atmosphere that is 'relaxed, informal and friendly' (Stone, 1981, 190).

Such schools are justifiably proud of their independence from a state education system which many black parents and teachers see as having failed their pupils. It is not surprising, therefore, that successful supplementary schools, having developed as self-help groups, are wary of risking their autonomy by receiving financial backing from official sources. In seeking to support supplementary schools, local education authorities and individual mainstream schools should realize that the strength of the supplementary school movement lies in its independence. By showing a willingness to learn from this independent tradition, those involved in mainstream education might eventually learn how to work alongside it in a spirit of equal partnership. There is certainly a great deal to be learnt from the aims and practices of supplementary schools, in terms of parental involvement, curriculum content and teaching methods, and pupil/teacher relationships. A respect for, and understanding of, these achievements is a prerequisite of effective dialogue between mainstream and supplementary education.

At the heart of the supplementary school movement is a desire to equip young people with what Richard Johnson (1979), in a rather different context, has referred to as 'really useful knowledge'. This phrase – central to the aims of radical education in the first half of the nineteenth century – expressed the conviction 'that real knowledge served practical ends, ends, that is, for the knower' (Johnson, 1979, 84). It was a way, on the one hand, of distancing working-class education from immediate instrumentalist aims and, on the other, of distinguishing it from merely recreational pursuits. Similarly, the recent development of supplementary schooling among minority ethnic groups is a demand for fully comprehensive education; education, that is, that is both widely available and extensive in content. Such an education should equip young people, not only with the skills necessary to cope within the world of work, but also with the necessary self-determination and sense of human agency to participate actively in every aspect of adult life.

Where it is an oppressed group that is acquiring this 'really useful knowledge', education necessarily becomes a political activity. Ultimately, therefore, teachers have to decide whose side they are on. The notion of 'community', as I have stressed throughout this chapter, can be a misleading one if it is taken to imply a lack of deep social divisions. A community which is devoid of social justice is no community at all. As a first step towards bridging the accountability gap, schools must acknowledge, in their practices and policies, that there can be no neutrality in the struggle against racism. 'If we are not for oppression', Barbara Rogers reminds us, 'then we must fight against it, with solidarity between the oppressed and those who wish to abandon the corruption of being the oppressor' (Rogers, 1980, 91). The relationship between schools, parents and community should be based upon precisely that principle.

To sum up. This chapter has argued that teachers cannot afford to rely upon legislative reorganization of the school governing body as a means of creating closer links between school and community. Such reorganization places undue emphasis on the power of parent governors, many of whom are unrepresentative of the community as a whole. If schools genuinely seek to forge closer relationships with the community, they must ensure that all parents have access to individual teachers and to any information pertaining to their children that is held in school files. They must also find ways of acting with the community on issues of immediate concern to parents and pupils. Some of these concerns – such as the undue proportion of black youths stopped on the street by the police and the impact of rising unemployment on black and working-class families – have barely begun to work their way onto the agenda of the mainstream school. It is to supplementary schools, therefore, that teachers need to look for a new model of partnership between school and community. In doing so they will have to call to account their own practice and that of the institutions in which they work. This process of self-critical appraisal – its methods, assumptions, and implications for the role of the teacher – is the focus of the next chapter.

CHAPTER EIGHT

Evaluation and Development

Implicit in the argument so far is the assumption that evaluation and development are twin aspects of a single process: education for a multicultural society relies, in other words, on teachers having the willingness and expertise to appraise their own practice and on schools offering the support necessary for them to be able to do so. The present chapter explores this assumption in more detail by looking at the nature of evaluation, its methods and the kinds of impact it might have on educational policy and practice. In so doing it draws on a tradition within the field of curriculum studies (see, for example, Harlen, 1978; Nixon, 1981; and Stenhouse, 1975) that has stressed the role of the teacher as a researcher; a role characterized, according to the late Lawrence Stenhouse, by its 'capacity for autonomous professional self-development through systematic self-study, through the study of the work of other teachers and through the testing of ideas of classroom research procedures' (Stenhouse, 1975, 144).

In drawing on this tradition I am not suggesting that a solution to problems experienced in the classroom can be found simply be looking at them as classroom problems. Far from it. Educational enquiry, as described in the following pages, involves seeing the classroom in its social and political setting; grasping, that is, the dynamics of the relation between case and context. Nor am I suggesting that such enquiry offers a cheap option for schools and local education authorities. On the contrary, it costs dear in terms of staffing, timetabling, and intellectual energy. My only claim for it is that it increases teachers' understanding, both of their own practice and of the principles underlying that practice. As such it can help create a context more conducive to change.

ACTION AND REFLECTION

This point needs stressing as it is often assumed that the impact of evaluation on practice and policy is immediate and direct. Where evaluation does change the practical structures of schooling, however, it is invariably because it has first had an effect on the mental constructs of those who are responsible for these structures. The impact of evaluation is primarily long-term and is felt at the level of indirect influence. Its direct influence, although more immediate, cannot be guaranteed.

Conceding this point in fact allows us to make a larger claim for in-school evaluation. Insofar as it alters the context of ideas in which teachers operate, its impact can be felt beyond the immediate environment in which it is conducted. The insights culled from classroom evaluation can contribute to a cumulative altering of perceptions that has repercussions far beyond the confines of the classroom. Its impact is felt in the way in which it informs staffroom talk, challenges colleagues' assumptions, and places certain issues on the agenda of the school.

Moreover, this indirect, if far-reaching, influence may in turn lead to direct intervention at the levels of policy and practice. In such cases there is the possibility of improving, not only the practice of individual teachers, but also the context within which that practice occurs. The importance of in-school evaluation is considerable, therefore, in terms of both the professional development of teachers and the efficiency of the school as a whole.

Its potential in these areas is summarized in Figure 4. The cells of this matrix do not, it should be noted, represent different kinds of evaluation, but different possibilities inherent in a process that involves both evaluation and development. Once underway, that process produces a ripple effect which may, under favourable circumstances, lead to broad institutional change. Under less favourable circumstances, the extent of the ripple effect is uncertain and unpredictable. What is clear, however, is the central importance, in any attempt at institutional change, of teachers understanding their own practice.

	Case	Context
Reflection	Increased understanding of individual practice by the teacher concerned.	Increased understanding of collective practice by a group of teachers or the staff as a whole.
Action	Improvement in individual practice.	Improvement in collective practice.

Figure 4 *The potential of in-school evaluation*

Teachers who have been involved in classroom evaluation have pointed to their own increased understanding and self-awareness as being one of its main areas of impact. The following comments, for example, made by practising teachers, stress the importance of evaluation as a means of prompting critical self-appraisal within the school:

It has made me think twice about the things I say and do in the classroom ... It enabled me to discover more about myself as a teacher. (Enright, 1981, 51)

Really taking control of and caring about the quality of what is going on in your classroom leads some teachers into seeing themselves as active initiators rather than child managers. (Jackson, 1981, 60)

We found the activity of research to be both educative and humanising. (James and Ebbutt, 1981, 94)

The department and school benefit by being formally told about the research and by the research being talked about and used as evidence in many different contexts, whether it be informally in the staffroom or in curriculum planning meetings. (Smiddy, 1981, 120)

The claims made by these teachers for the kinds of enquiry they have undertaken chime in well with one of the major themes of the continuing debate within multicultural education. The need for teachers to reappraise the principles underlying their own practice and to take a critical look at their own attitudes concerning ethnic minority groups was clearly spelt out in the Rampton Report, a controversial section of which dealt with racism as a major factor contributing to the underachievement of West Indian children as a group within the education system. 'Teachers should be prepared', the report argued, 'to examine and reappraise their own attitudes and actions in an effort to ensure that their behaviour towards and expectations of ethnic minority pupils are not influenced by stereotyped and negative views' (Department of Education and Science, 1981, 14).

Although referring specifically to the treatment of West Indian children in schools, this recommendation has implications for the education of all pupils within a multicultural society. For the transmission of 'stereotyped and negative views' by teachers is harmful whether or not the school has a multiracial intake. What the recommendation does in fact is to place the professional self-awareness of teachers at the centre of the debate about multicultural education. Insofar as the growth of this awareness is fostered by teachers adopting an evaluation stance to their work, the kinds of self-monitoring procedures discussed in the following pages might be seen as potential means of informing the school's overall response to pupils' needs.

PRINCIPLES AND PROCEDURES

Teachers attempting to realize this potential will almost certainly face the initial and perhaps continuing problem of resistance from colleagues. This resistance may be in part an unwillingness to take on what may be considered a time-consuming task requiring the acquisition of new skills and expertise. It may, also, be in part a worry about the uses to which the 'findings' of the evaluation may be put by other teachers, by community groups and by employers. Both aspects of the problem are understandable and need to be confronted directly.

With regard to teachers' uncertainty concerning their own skills and the time available, it should be understood from the outset that what is being advocated is a style of evaluation that builds on the existing strengths of the staff and operates within the constraints of the school. All teachers possess certain skills which can contribute to in-school evaluation. The important thing is to clarify and define one's own particular set of skills. Some teachers, for example, are able to collect and interpret statistical data; others to record in retrospective accounts the key moments of a lesson. One teacher may know something about questionnaire design; another have a natural flair for interviewing. It is essential that teachers work from their own particular strengths when evaluating the work of the school.

The situations within which teachers work are as varied as the skills they possess. Each situation, moreover, imposes its own set of constraints. Time is a crucial factor in this respect; but the availability of space and resources are also important. Some schools, for example, are equipped with the most up-to-date audio-visual equipment; others cannot even boast a cassette tape recorder. Some have spare rooms in which interviews could be carried out; others hardly have enough space to implement the existing timetable. If evaluation is to be anything other than a good intention, it must be designed in such a way as to be easily implemented within the pattern of constraints existing within the institution.

Those who conceive of evaluation in these terms are perhaps less likely to dismiss it as impracticable. There remains, however, the worry, entertained by many teachers, about the consequences that might ensue from others watching the teaching profession criticize itself and, even worse, from their possibly gaining access to detailed critiques of existing practice. Self-criticism, so the argument runs, leads to public condemnation. Is the urge towards evaluation, then, not simply a way of making teachers more accountable to heads, heads more accountable to local education authorities, and local education authorities to central government? Control, according to this analysis, is the key issue.

To some extent, of course, it is. That is why clear principles of procedure are essential in any evaluation exercise. The politics of schooling is always complex, in terms both of the relationships within the school and of the relations between school and society. Information gathered in the course of the evaluation is likely, therefore, to be sensitive and open to misuse. If teachers and pupils are to be afforded any protection, an agreed code of conduct is required with regard to such matters as access, the definition of boundaries, the release of data, and confidentiality.

Negotiated access. Access to colleagues' classrooms, to materials and resources, and to school records should be negotiated from the outset with all parties concerned. Permission or encouragement from the headteacher to carry out the evaluation is no substitute for negotiation with colleagues. Where the enquiry includes an analysis of pupil records or interviews with pupils, parents should be informed of the nature and purpose of the exercise and given the opportunity of opting out on their child's behalf. (See Simons, 1981, for a detailed discussion of the principles governing research interviews in schools.)

Negotiation of boundaries. The boundaries of an evaluation study are defined not only by its site and sources, but also by the kinds of questions one hopes to address in the course of the enquiry. These questions should relate to the practical concerns of the staff; concerns which can only be ascertained through discussion and negotiation. Without such negotiation there is little hope of building a context in which the evaluation may eventually have far-reaching impact. Moreover, since the practical concerns of the teachers may shift in the course of the enquiry, the boundaries of the study may need to be modified through a continuing process of renegotiation.

Negotiation of release. The classic dilemma regarding any investigation undertaken on democratic principles is that between the individual's 'right to privacy' and the public's 'right to know'. In the case of in-school evaluation 'the public' is a comprehensive category including parents, pupils, teachers and employers. Where any discussion of 'unintentional racism' is concerned, the 'right to know' is arguably very strong. However, there is little point in 'going public' with an evaluation until the participants have themselves had the opportunity to learn from it. A system of controlled release is a possible compromise. This would involve renegotiation between all the participants at each new stage of 'going public'.

Confidentiality. Confidentiality is a notoriously difficult principle to observe within the comparatively small community of a school. Yet without that principle, any evaluation exercise is likely to defeat its own ends by dividing the staff and creating an atmosphere of mistrust and even hostility. Information relating to the attitudes and behaviour of specific individuals, whether pupils or teachers, should never be collected covertly. Nor should it be passed on to others without the express permission of the person concerned. Anonymity is not a particularly effective means of concealing the identity of colleagues or pupils, since contextual clues can more than compensate for the lack of a name. Under certain circumstances silence may be the only way of respecting a confidence.

The purpose of these procedural principles is not to safeguard teachers from the consequences of their own 'unintentional racism'. It is, rather, to create a working environment in which they can feel sufficiently secure to learn from one another, from their pupils, and from the local community. The purpose, in other words, is to build a collaborative context in which structural change becomes a real option.

For this very reason in-school evaluation will be resisted by those who are afraid or mistrustful of curriculum innovation. Among the fearful must be numbered those whose assumptions are, openly or implicitly, assimilationist and who therefore see no reason for change: as far as this group is concerned the kinds of arguments outlined at the end of chapter 3 remain the only persuasive strategy. Among the mistrustful are those who, notwithstanding their own involvement in schooling, believe change to be possible only outside the institutions and therefore see curriculum innovation as being ineffectual: the point at issue here is not whether racism exists in schools, but how it might be confronted and eradicated within society at large.

A common charge against the evaluation movement is that it has tried to understand schools when the point is to change them. It is a charge that rides on the back of a false dichotomy. For institutional racism is not something which exists 'out there' as a kind of cancerous growth to be located in the body politic and then burnt out. It is part of our own thinking and our own patterns of response. It emerges in the minutiae of our interpersonal relationships and social interactions. A sustained and reasoned appraisal of our own social practice is, ultimately, the only effective means of confronting racism and bringing about lasting change in the structure of society.

For those who are willing to embark upon the task of in-school evaluation, the single most pressing problem is that of finding a focus for the study. Before any fieldwork is undertaken, it is necessary to agree on a broad area of concern and to break this down into a specific structure of issues. This structure will serve to inform the ensuing evaluation, providing a loose framework for collecting, sifting and analysing the evidence. It may take the form of a 'checklist' of questions, a 'schedule' of categories, or a series of 'foreshadowed problems'; it may evolve through discussion, derive from previously disseminated material, or be achieved through a combination of both. The purpose of this focusing procedure, it should be noted, is not to generate a set of hypotheses which can then be tested, but to open up key areas of concern for future exploration and analysis.

AREAS OF CONCERN

This stress on the need for an agreed focus of issues ought not to be taken as a suggestion that, within any particular area of concern, the key issues will remain static. Frames of reference shift rapidly within the debate on multicultural education. Not only do the issues themselves change, but there is also a swift turnover in terminology; each new term applying a slightly different semantic shading. The task for any team of teacher/ evaluators is to remain responsive to these changing currents, while at the same time keeping on course as far as the broad boundaries of the study are concerned.

Three areas of particular concern can be distinguished within the field of multicultural education: classroom procedures, learning materials, and school organization. These have produced their own distinct modes of investigation and their own specific sets of issues. The following points suggest starting points for evaluation work within these areas.

Classroom observation

When the focus of attention is on classroom procedures, as these relate either to the act of teaching or to the pupils' learning, some form of classroom observation is appropriate. I am using the term 'observation' loosely here to refer to any attempt on behalf of teachers to 'see' their classrooms afresh. This may involve having a colleague in one's own classroom to comment upon what is happening; but, equally, it can be conducted by individual teachers studying tapes of their own lessons, taking detailed notes on a particular aspect of their own teaching, or interviewing pupils about the work.

In any classroom observation exercise of this kind it should be borne in mind that there can be no single correct way of seeing the classroom; no less through which the teacher may gaze to achieve a full image of actuality. Each lesson is a complex web of messages and signals in which the teacher no less than the pupils is inextricably entwined. The object of the exercise is to find ways of seeing the classroom from new and surprising angles. Teachers need to transcend the limitations of their own teacherly perspective if they are to learn about the fits and starts, the circuitous routes, by which their pupils learn.

The methods employed in classroom observation fall broadly into four categories, each of which raises important procedural points:

The role of observer may vary from that of partner in a virtual team-teaching situation to that of a non-participant presence in the classroom. Where the observer is located on this particular continuum depends to a very large extent on prior negotiations with the teacher concerned. The notion of a negotiated contract between observer and teacher is an extremely important element in the classroom evaluation process. Indeed, without some prior negotiation as to what the observer will be looking at, the experience may not only be unhelpful for the teacher but downright disturbing.

Tape recording of lessons may be problematical in particular kinds of teaching situations. Given only a standard cassette recorder it might be necessary to make a selection of what to record and when: if small-group work is in progress, it may be useful to deposit the recorder with one particular group; where there is a considerable amount of movement around the classroom, record just those moments when it is possible to pick out individual voices. In such situations the teacher should plan ahead regarding those phases of the lesson that might be recorded. Bearing in mind that the purpose of the recording is to improve one's own understanding, tape only what is relevant to the focus of the study and, even then, only what there is time to analyse.

Diary accounts are used to obtain an overview of the lesson as a whole and to analyse in detail particular parts of the lesson in relation to prespecified themes and issues. In my own attempts at self-monitoring I have found it useful to produce two kinds of retrospective accounts: one, written very shortly after the lesson, recording immediate impressions and ideas; and the other, a more reflective account, written a few days later. Phasing the written response in this way allows one to check considered judgements against 'gut reactions'. There is a danger in any personal account of telling it, not as it was, but as one would like it to have been. By recording an immediate response to the lesson, the teacher can work towards an interpretation that is grounded in the reality of the classroom.

Interviews may take a variety of forms: observer interviews teacher, teacher interviews pupil(s), pupil interviews teacher, pupil interviews pupil, observer interviews pupil. The most common form, however, is the teacher interviewing the pupil. The problem in this case is to create a sufficiently relaxed and secure atmosphere for the pupil to talk frankly to the teacher about the lesson. One way of achieving this sense of security is to establish at the outset that pupils have control over anything they may say in the interview. With this in mind they should be given the opportunity of listening to the tape after the interview and erasing any of their own remarks if they so wish. On no occasion should pressure be put on a pupil to take part in an interview; those that are willing to participate should be given the option of being interviewed separately or as a group.

The use of a combination of these methods is preferable to an exclusive reliance on any one of them. Not only does a multi-method approach offer a fuller and more complex portrayal of the classroom, but it also operates as a check against the tilt and bias – the 'method boundedness' – of the various techniques employed. An interpretation based, for example, on an observer's account, interviews with pupils and the teacher's own field notes is likely to be more reliable and authoritative than an interpretation which draws upon a single source. The term 'triangulation' is sometimes used to describe this process of combining distinct methods of classroom observation. For, like the tradition of orientation from which the term is taken, a combined approach involves ascertaining and understanding the relations between differently placed referents.

No methodological system should be adopted for its own sake, however. Classroom observation – even when used to monitor a specific, clearly defined intervention – is an interpretive activity: it involves teachers in an attempt to understand the meaning of their own classrooms. The procedures adopted are of value, therefore, only insofar as they inform this interpretive task. The design of the evaluation must above all be practicable as far as both the school and the participants are concerned. An obsession with methodological rigour is one of the great enemies of intellectual seriousness.

Reviewing materials

Another equally important area of concern is the racist bias of many of the materials used in schools. A thorough review of the book stock, the purchasing policy of the school, and the library organization is essential if the extent of this bias is to be fully understood. In fact, a considerable amount of work has already been done in this area (see, for example, Dixon, 1977; Jones and Klein, 1980; Klein, 1982; and National Union of Teachers, 1979), with the result that teachers now have a variety of checklists and guidelines to draw on when beginning to evaluate materials used in school.

The following, relating specifically to book stock, serves as a useful example of the kinds of questions teachers are often asked to consider when embarking upon an evaluation of this kind:

- Do the books in the library reflect the children in the school?
- Do the books reflect the cultural diversity of British society today?
- Are the books evaluated with regard to their messages on issues of race, sex and class?
- Is there a working party composed of the librarian and teachers in the school re-examining the library books?
- Are there still racist books on the shelves?
- How long ago were the history and geography background reading books on the shelves published?
- What do you do with the books you withdraw?
- Are there books about anti-racist leaders, white and black?
- Do you stock books in the mother-tongues of the pupils (if such books can be found)?
- Where are the mother-tongue books (if any) shelved?

– Do you carry a range of periodicals that relate to ethnic minority groups, including music journals? (Klein, 1981, 4)

A number of these questions are effective as initial prompts to action. Beyond that purely rhetorical function, however, they remain severely limited. The trouble with these questions is that they over-simplify the complexity and subtlety of the evaluative task. The assumption underlying them is that racist bias is limited to certain texts which can be recognized as racist by the teacher or librarian. Of course, with blatant examples of racism this recognition may be relatively uncomplicated. Where racism operates most effectively, though, is at the subliminal level. It reproduces and reinforces dominant definitions and categories which form part of our everyday social knowledge and are therefore rarely questioned. 'The problem', as David Wright points out, 'is that we are the products of a society which has not adequately examined its own values and assumptions, and we are not yet skilled at spotting racism and bias' (Wright, 1983, 5).

This problem, which is essentially one of racism awareness, cannot be met adequately by simply censoring those texts which are considered racist. The point here is a pragmatic, not an ethical one: racism, as ideology, is not restricted to particular texts and so cannot be eradicated by any 'burning of the books' policy. It may in fact be least dangerous when stated most explicitly; in its inarticulated practices it remains powerfully influential. What is needed is an attitude of critical enquiry whereby pupils and teachers come to recognize the implicit racism of the texts and visual images which confront them in and outside school. Given that the creation of a non-racist library or stock room is at best a long-term aim, the immediate purpose of such an enquiry must be to develop an anti-racist readership.

A more useful checklist of questions, therefore, would be one which highlighted the possible distortions in all texts and helped teachers to think about how they might raise their pupils' awareness of these distortions. Dave Hicks includes such a checklist as an appendix to his study of bias in geography textbooks (Hicks, 1980). The following questions from that list are particularly appropriate to the needs of the self-evaluating teacher:

- Do I have the sensitivity to explain distortions and biases in a manner which will raise the level of awareness of my students?
- Do I have methods to develop honest exploration and understanding of the topic and attitudes of respect for the identity of others?
- Can I use concrete situations in the classroom and relationships among students as a point of departure to illustrate the origin of distortions and biases reflected in the text?
- Since there is no totally unbiased text, can I use a racially biased text to show how distortions can be propogated?
- Am I sensitive enough to point out overt, crude, racist statements about others but also to discover the more subtle covert forms of racial presentation?
- Can I handle racist material sufficiently well to affect real life situations outside the classroom and to counteract the effects of the children's own reading and the effects of the media?
- Am I willing to search out information which would actively counteract the effects of the children's own reading and the effects of the media? (ibid., 42)

The advantage of these questions is that they lead to a close examination of teaching materials within the classroom situation. A preliminary task may well be the sort of in-depth critique that has recently been undertaken by Dawn Gill in her review of the Schools Council Geography for the Young School Leaver Course (Gill, 1982). However, unless valuable work of this kind serves to inform classroom discussion, its impact is likely to be extremely limited. Less ambitious in scope than that carried out by Gill, a project developed in a Berkshire primary school by Peter Ranson nevertheless points a useful way forward (Ranson, 1983). Having selected a particular published text designed to assess and extend the reading skills of the pupil, he decided not to formulate his own critique of it but to investigate his pupils' reactions and to probe with them any cultural differences in interpretation which he and they experienced. This he did by interviewing the pupils, tape-recording their replies and analysing these. His conclusion comes as no surprise: 'for a piece of writing to be relevant or fully comprehended the children needed to have some concrete experience related to what was in print' (ibid., 42). In the process of confirming this insight, though, he himself gained a much clearer and more sympathetic understanding of the pupils' own responses to the text. They in turn benefited from their involvement in the evaluation process by learning to recognize and challenge distortions and bias in their reading materials.

Monitoring the school

A third area of concern requiring careful evaluation includes those organizational elements of school life which, because they cannot be restricted to a particular classroom or a specific set of materials, may all too easily be overlooked. Their effects on the life chances of individual pupils are, nevertheless, highly significant. The monitoring of pupil achievement across the range of subjects together with an analysis of the formal and informal assessment procedures used within the school are a major priority in this area. Marten Shipman's work, although not directly related to the concerns of multicultural education, is particularly relevant to this perspective. For he sees the task of evaluation as including an ongoing review`of what he calls the 'school assessment programme' together with the 'wider aspects of school life' (Shipman, 1979). This brief section focuses on one of the most important of those aspects: the public examination system.

The concern expressed by the black community itself at the underachievement of West Indian chidren in British schools places the public examination system at the centre of often fierce controversy. As early as 1978 the Black Peoples Progressive Association in Redbridge pointed out that 'many West Indian pupils in Redbridge are underachieving and the level of that underachievement is extremely worrying' (Black People Progress Association, 1978, 10). More recently, in 1983, the Haringey Black Pressure Group on Education called on the local education authority to instruct all headteachers to report within four weeks on a number of areas of pressing concern. This demand included specific reference to the need for information on how headteachers 'intend to improve the overall performance and results in O level examinations, including an increase in the number of black pupils who are entered for O levels' (Black Pressure Group on Education, 1983).

While, as the Rampton Report pointed out, the onus is upon examining boards to 'undertake a systematic review of the relevance of their syllabuses to the needs of today's multiracial school population' (Department of Education and Science, 1981, 79), there is also a great deal that teachers can do in the way of evaluating the examinations in use in schools. At a conference held at the Schools Council in 1981, a number of teachers came together with representatives from various examining boards to discuss issues relating to the evaluation of examinations in a multicultural society. This group highlighted the need for examinations which are culturally fairer for ethnic minority pupils and put forward the following questions as starting points for evaluating current practice:

- Is there, within the examinations, a variety of forms of assessment (projects, coursework, etc.) to enable teachers to encourage pupils to use skills or follow up interests which arise from particular cultural backgrounds?
- Does the language, particularly the figurative and idiomatic, used for examination questions, minimise difficulties of comprehension?
- Are examiners sensitive to the difficulties candidates can have in demonstrating their abilities, if their first language is not English? Is marking empathetic to candidates, rewarding attainment demonstrated through various cultural forms and responsive to the full range of acceptable language? (Schools Council, 1981, 18)

It was not only the need for fairer examining of ethnic minority pupils that was stressed at this conference, however. The participants also called for more culturally diverse examinations for all candidates. A balance within syllabuses between compulsory and optional components was favoured, such that a multicultural approach might be included as a core element (as in a number of World History syllabuses) and also as an area of specialization for pupils with particular interests (for example, optional West Indian history). Moreover, it was stressed that this culturally broader selection of knowledge should be reflected in the examination paper and not just in the syllabus content. Where this would be difficult using the traditional single paper examination, other forms of assessment should, it was argued, be developed.

Clearly, teachers are not responsible for the overall range of public examinations on offer in any given subject area. They are very largely responsible, however, for the kinds of examinations offered within their own school. A serious review of past papers and course work assignments undertaken by an interdisciplinary team of teachers can fulfil two useful functions: it can alert teachers within a particular school or across a community of schools to the limitations of their formal assessment programme and, by so doing, can begin to exert, through subject panels and direct representation, pressure upon the examining boards to revise their syllabuses and examination procedures.

The examination system is by no means the only wider aspect of school life in need of careful monitoring. Non-academic and extra-curricular activities, pupil-absence patterns, the staying-on rates of different groups of pupils beyond the statutory leaving age, and the destination of school leavers are all important aspects in need of some form of ongoing evaluation. The examination system remains, however, at the centre of the concern felt by black parents and educationists about the education of their children. Moreover, the current plans for a new 16+ examination system, together with Sir Keith Joseph's recent call for a clarification of criteria in each subject area, could be seen as a prime opportunity for reviewing the basic values and priorities upon which the public assessment of all pupils is based. Teachers should have a vital part to play in any such review.

SUPPORT FOR DEVELOPMENT

The three areas of concern just outlined are, of course, complementary and overlapping. Teachers seriously attempting to evaluate their own practice in terms of the issues raised in this book would need, therefore, to develop frameworks for observing their own and others' classrooms, reviewing the materials and resources available, and monitoring the wider aspects of school life. In order to do this they would have to be sure of the necessary support from both inside and outside the school. Without that support in-school evaluation, as anything other than occasional one-off initiatives taken by isolated enthusiasts, is impossible to sustain.

By way of conclusion to this chapter, therefore, we shall glance briefly at the kinds of support necessary for teachers to adopt an evaluative stance to their work. The first of these is the school itself. Here the moral support of the headteacher and deputies is of central importance. For they exert a strong influence on the ethos of the school and thereby on its capacity for self-criticism and development. Where innovations lack the active moral support of the headteacher, they rarely, regardless of the strength of support from elsewhere, have much impact on policy and practice within the school itself.

Moral support, however, is not enough. In-school evaluation also requires practical support in the form of flexible time-tabling and resource provision. Those evaluating their own practice need time, both for data collection and analysis. In the case of classroom observation in particular provision should be made for teachers to observe one another and to discuss their observations. There ought to be no assumption that this can be carried out during non-teaching time or after school. If headteachers take seriously the notion of the school as a self-evaluating community, they must provide time within which teachers can evaluate their work over and above their normal duties.

They must also be willing to provide the necessary resources. These range from relatively inexpensive items of hardware, such as cassette recorders and tapes, to more expensive human resources. John Smiddy has documented an interesting experiment at Hackney Downs School, a secondary school in north London, whereby one member of staff was, for a short time, released from the daily pressures of teaching so as to be able to observe colleagues teaching in the humanities faculty and pinpoint key issues for discussion within the faculty (Smiddy, 1981). A more ambitiuos project was set up in a Leicestershire primary school where two teachers, Michael Armstrong and Stephen Rowland, worked together for a whole year with a single class, documenting the intellectual growth and development of the pupils (Armstrong, 1980 and 1981). Both these projects were expensive in terms of human resources and the second one in particular is probably beyond the financial scope of all but a few primary schools. In any school where classroom observation is considered, however, it should be realized that enquiries of this kind cost money.

There is an obvious lesson here for local and central government: cuts in public expenditure on education invariably lead to a lowering of professional standards in schools. No amount of rhetoric by politicians about the need for schools to define the criteria by which they are to assess pupils within given subject areas can compensate for the lack of resources which renders the clarification of these criteria a virtual impossibility. If the education of pupils for a multicultural society is important, then the value placed upon it must be reflected in the nation's budget.

This brings us to the second kind of support necessary for teachers to adopt an evaluative stance to their work; namely, the wider educational context. Here the part played by teachers' centres and local resource projects is of paramount importance. These provide an opportunity for teachers, not only to share their knowledge of different classrooms, but to develop the necessary skills for in-school evaluation and to disseminate the results of their own studies across a community of schools. In the emphasis that has rightly been given to school-focused in-service education in recent years it should be remembered that teachers still require off-site support. Teachers cannot develop themselves professionally without reference to the work of colleagues in other schools and to expertise drawn from other institutions.

Higher education in particular has a vital role to play in providing the necessary links and networks for teachers to be able to share their experiences in this way. Far too often, however, there is little effort to coordinate the in-service work carried out by such institutions with the work of teachers' centres and that of the local advisory service. In the field of initial teacher training the lack of coordination and overall planning is even more apparent. The question of support raises crucial issues relating to the initial and in-service training of teachers. These issues are the focus of the following chapter.

Evaluation, ultimately, is concerned with the consideration of values. Professional development cannot be divorced from the personal development of teachers; there can, in other words, be no change in a teacher unless the person who is that teacher also changes. A growing awareness by teachers of the assumptions underlying their own practice, together with their gradual articulation of the value system upon which the aims of their educational practice is based, is the heart of the matter. 'Teachers', as Jennifer Nias puts it, 'march to the sound of a more distant drummer than legislators or administrators may think or teacher educators hope' (Nias, 1984, 15).

To sum up. This chapter has outlined some of the principles and procedures of a mode of evaluation which aims to changing the structure of schooling by developing the understanding of teachers. Three areas of concern have been defined as particularly relevant to this perspective: (1) the observation of classroom procedures; (2) the analysis of classroom materials; and (3) monitoring the wider aspects of schooling. Finally, the need for support has been stressed; both from inside the school and from within the wider context of schooling. A key element in this wider context is the initial and in-service education of teachers. In the final chapter we shall explore the theme of teacher education in greater detail.

CHAPTER NINE

Teacher Education

Teacher education is passing through a state of turmoil and insecurity. Cuts in public expenditure have reduced staff to a bare minimum, while the 1983 White Paper, which effectively limits the role of the teacher educator to that of teacher trainer, has done little to raise the morale of those who remain. It is not enough, therefore, merely to argue for the inclusion on teacher education courses of a multicultural education component covering the kinds of issues raised in the previous chapters. If those working in institutions of higher education are to equip their students to teach in a multicultural society, they must look critically, across the full range of academic disciplines, professional skills and organizational structures, at the principles underlying their own practice. The quality of tomorrow's schooling will depend on the willingness of teacher educators to take on this evaluative task and the readiness of central and local government to support them.

INSTITUTIONAL CONSTRAINTS

A superficial reading of the 1983 White Paper would suggest that the Secretaries of State for Education are prepared, not only to support, but to initiate such a review of teacher education. Their paper was a clear statement of their intention to publish criteria to which all existing approved courses of initial teacher education will have to conform. These criteria, it was stressed, will impose certain broad requirements on those responsible for such courses. One such requirement, specified in the White Paper, is 'that the initial teacher training of all qualified teachers should include studies linked with practical experience in schools' (Department of Education and Science, 1983, 19). In order that this requirement should be met, it was stipulated that the school experience of 'a sufficient proportion of each training institution's staff ... should be recent, substantial and relevant' (ibid., 20). On the face of it this demand would seem to be a laudable attempt to shift the emphasis within teacher education from purely academic, to school-focused, concerns.

Even the White Paper acknowledges, however, that the matter is not quite as simple as that. For few of the existing staff in institutions responsible for initial teacher education have anything approaching 'recent, substantial and relevant' school experience. As a result such experience is having to be 'bought in' on a short-term basis, either through secondments or, as is more often the case, through fixed-term contracts and part-time hours, while those who lack the necessary school experience take on an increasingly heavy administrative burden. The effect of this is to create a sharply divided, and divisive, two-tier staffing structure. On the one hand, those whose experience is mainly in teacher education become locked into their executive roles and, on the other hand, those who are brought in to innovate are unable to do so because they lack both an intimate knowledge of the system and also the necessary access to decision-making power. Under such circumstances curriculum development becomes little more than a series of sporadic bursts of energy by those hotfoot from the classroom, while overall control of the curriculum structure remains safely in the hands of those whose school experience is neither recent, substantial, nor particularly relevant. The consequences of imposing severe financial constraints on teacher education and at the same time demanding significant, and specific, changes in the staffing policies of particular institutions are likely, therefore, to be disastrous.

These consequences need to be spelt out since they relate specifically to the task of developing a teacher education programme that is responsive to the needs of a multicultural society:

Professional isolation. The kind of open dialogue that is essential to any effective curriculum development is virtually impossible to achieve between workers who, although contractually obliged to assume similar responsibilities, enjoy very different rights in terms of security of tenure. The notion of collaboration can have little significance in such a situation, until the underlying asymmetry of the relationships existing between professionals is acknowledged and seen to be a major obstacle in the way of change and development. A concerted effort must be made, at all levels, to create more equitable staffing arrangements. The only alternative to such an effort is a capitulation by all concerned to a continuing state of professional isolation.

Short-term goals. A further problem is that those who are employed on a short-term basis, whether on secondments, joint teacher-tutor appointments or schemes of teacher-tutor exchange (all specified within the White Paper as useful possibilities), are likely to operate in terms of short-term goals. Many, particularly those teaching on four-year B.Ed. courses, may not even see a single intake of student teachers through the initial teacher education programme. The result can only be a lack of any long-term, coordinated planning. Unless, that is, a plan is imposed from above by a senior management team; in which case it is likely to be singularly ineffective.

Discontinuity and inconsistency. The students, of course, are the victims of such a system. For them, a rapid turnover of staff is experienced as discontinuity; a lack of consultation between colleagues as inconsistency. This sense of dislocation can only serve to compound the problem. For any serious review of initial teacher education for a multicultural society should involve the students themselves in adopting an analytical and evaluative role. Without this involvement any attempt at curriculum review is likely to be serverely limited in its impact.

The picture I have painted may seem an unduly bleak one. It is to my mind, however, an accurate projection of what the 1983 White Paper holds in store for teacher education, unless those involved are prepared seriously to challenge some of its basic assumptions. Effective curriculum development must build upon genuine collaboration. In moving on to some of the key issues in teacher education for a multicultural society, this point should remain at the forefront of our considerations.

ACCESS TO TEACHER EDUCATION

One such issue is that of access to teacher education. Adequate research on the employment of ethnic minority teachers in Britain is as yet lacking. One small-scale enquiry carried out in 1980 estimated that there were only 800 teachers of West Indian origin currently working in British schools (Gibbes, 1980), but no detailed information is available on a national scale. Rhetoric, however, has more than compensated for the lack of hard evidence. The National Association for Teachers in Further and Higher Education, for example, has referred to the 'desperate urgency to increase as dramatically and quickly as possible the number of black teachers in Britain's schools' (House of Commons, 1981b, 148), while the Rampton Report has recommended that 'LEAs should seek to recruit more West Indian teachers and professionals and to ensure equal opportunities for them at all levels in the education service' (Department of Education and Science, 1981, 64).

As assumption underlying these statements is that the employment of more black teachers would be advantageous to schools. In particular, it would:

1 create closer links between black families and schools in multiracial areas;
2 present black pupils with role-models and useful points of contact within school;
3 help meet the special language needs of pupils from ethnic minority groups;
4 offer an important perspective in staff discussions concerning the education of pupils for a multicultural society; and
5 confront the institutional racism in schools whereby black teachers are denied access to posts of responsibility.

That last point is, I believe, the most important. Until schools confront the racism implicit in their own staffing structures any attempt at curriculum development in the area of multicultural education will have miminal impact.

Responding to public concern over the disproportionately low numbers of teachers from the ethnic minorities in schools, the Department of Education and Science in 1978 invited seven local education authorities to set up pilot schemes to establish special access link courses. These were designed to prepare students, particularly mature students, from minority ethnic groups to enter teaching and other professions. A letter sent from the Department of Education and Science to the Chief Education Officers of Avon, Bedfordshire, Birmingham, Haringey, ILEA, Leicestershire and Manchester education authorities couched the invitation in the following terms:

> It is part of the Government's policy to ensure that all members of the community have equal opportunities to develop their aptitudes and abilities to the full and, in particular, to encourage the entry into the professions and responsible posts in worthwhile careers of those whose background or experience could prove valuable, but who lack the requisite qualifications for entry to the appropriate training course. To reinforce this policy, the Government hopes that preparator courses, designed to bring such students up to the standard required for entry to higher education generally, can be developed. (Department of Education and Science, 1978)

In addition to undertaking academic study of one or more subjects to a level suitable for entry to higher education, potential students would, the letter stated, 'need to develop skills in study and in numeracy and communication to broaden and deepen their general education background' (ibid.).

Special access courses have now established a strong momentum. Their range, and the number of staff and students involved in them, have increased significantly since 1978. These courses have an attractive diversity. It would be difficult to find a general consensus about recruitment, selection, course objectives and assessment. Yet beneath this diversity lie some common assumptions. These were spelt out in the report on a DES conference on 'Access Courses to Higher Education':

> There is a professional concern to help disadvantaged students to learn to study, to discipline powers of communication, to see the relevance of hard-won experience to academic investigation and possible vocations, to meet unfamiliar challenges in counselling and to work out, ab initio, how best to work with, and to respond to, an institute of higher education, which is both partner and tune-caller. (Department of Education and Science, 1980, 29)

There was also agreement among the conference participants that an English and Mathematics Ordinary Level GCE requiremet can generate tension among students, disproportionate to the place of these studies within the whole course.

One such course, linked to the B.Ed. degree course at Middlesex Polytechnic, was set up at Paddington Further Education College in September 1979. The course has two main categories: core subjects (which comprise English, Mathematics, and Study and Communication Skills) and topics (comprising Drama, Literature, Philosophy, Psychology and Politics). The topics are intended to familiarize students with concepts and issues relevant to each of the disciplines raher than impose a narrow focus of study upon them. Two hours a week are spent in tutorials, one of which is devoted to personal counselling. A pre-vocational element is also provided in the form of visits to schools. It may well be – as Cliff Crellin, who helped set up the experiment at the teacher education end, has claimed – that a 'custom-built' course of this kind is a 'more suitable preparation for techer training than the more generalized "A" level course of the standard entrant' (Crellin, 1982, 15).

My own, albeit limited, experience as a teacher educator concerned with the Paddington College/Middlesex Polytechnic link is that insufficient attention has been paid, by the teacher educators, to the continuing support of 'access' students. Most of those whom I have taught have been exceptionally hardworking, well informed and politically aware. They have brought to their B.Ed. studies an intellectual vibrancy and breadth of experience that has been appreciated both by their peers and by the teaching staff. Where problems do arise, however, lecturers in higher education should be willing and able to extend their role to advise on such matters as study skills and literacy. This, in my experience, has not always been the case. A close and continuing relationship between further and higher education is essential if special access link courses are to fulfil their stated aims.

It is arguable whether the access link courses are an expression of what is often referred to as 'positive discrimination'. After all, the courses are externally examined so as to ensure that successful candidates have the capacity to profit from a higher education course. In that respect the 'access' student is in the same position as the student who enters teacher education by the conventional route. Moreover, the rationale for these courses is based as much upon the need for more black teachers as it is upon the special needs of the students themselves. Since, however, the establishing of access link courses is associated with other policies less ambiguously linked to the notion of 'positive discrimination', the controversy surrounding that notion needs to be briefly examined.

This is not the place to trace the history of positive discrimination in detail from Section 11 of the 1966 Local Government Act, through the setting up of the Educational Priority Areas and the Urban Aid Programme, to the more recent local government initiatives. It is important to note, however, that this history has its critics: policies based on the designation of particular areas as 'deprived' have been criticized on the ground that many – if not most – of those who are disadvantaged are thereby excluded (Barnes and Lucas, 1975); while policies based on the designation of particular ethnic minority groups as 'disadvantaged' have been dismissed on the ground that many of those who are not in fact disadvantaged are thereby included. Arguing this last case, Robert Jeffcoate has claimed that there is 'little evidence on how, or whether, racism impinges upon the educational prospects of children from the ethnic minorities' and that, as a result, 'there are no grounds for positive discrimination in favour of ethnic minorities as such.' Local authority initiatives to promote equality of opportunity for such groups are acceptable, states Jeffcoate, 'only insofar as they are limited to children who actually are immigrants and/or cannot speak English well enough to participate fully in the regular curriculum, and provided they are not separatist' (Jeffcoate, 1984, 75–95).

The alternative view – that there are strong grounds for positive discrimination in favour of ethnic minority groups as such – has been clearly stated by A.E. Halsey:

> The low performing black child is a fact. But the depression of a black community is not simply the sum of individual low performances. Theirs is a separate world within which individuals still vary, but around lower averages – a world socially determined by a complex set of discriminatory attitudes and policies which reinforce one another in limiting opportunities, effort and ambition. (Halsey, 1977, 144)

That notion of 'a separate world within which individuals still vary' is of central importance. There is no suggestion here that members of ethnic minority groups are homogeneous. What is being affirmed is that black people in Britain are subject to a unique 'set of discriminatory attitudes and policies'. In the case of certain individuals these may be ameliorated by class status or intensified by the effects of sexism. Nevertheless, racial discrimination pertains at all levels of social stratification.

Lurking behind the controversy is the question of what criteria should be used in assessing the need for positive discrimination. Jeffcoate, in denying the general effects of racism, is advocating an unnecessarily limited set of criteria. On the other hand, to build an entire system of positive discrimination around the notion of 'racial disadvantage' is equally limiting. The indices should incorporate the triple oppression of race, class and gender. Otherwise, as Lewis Killian has warned, 'the "new class" within the minority groups get better off while their lower-class fellows contend, with great justification, that they are worse of than before' (Killian, 1981, 16–17). One segment of the minority thus develops a vested interest in continuing the policy while another can only demand the enlargement of the programme.

In making this point I am in no way denying the need for more black teachers in schools, but simply relating this need to a broader debate about equal opportunities. The emphasis on access as an issue in this debate is not limited to teacher education. It is a key issue throughout the teaching profession: not only are there too few black teachers in positions of authority but also, to a lesser degree, too few women (particularly in certain subject areas) and too few men and women of whatever ethnic group who have come from working-class backgrounds. Too see these inequalities as being all of a piece is not to diminish their individual importance. It is merely to acknowledge that inequality relates, as R.H. Tawney pointed out, 'not to this or that specific characteristic of a group, but to a totality of conditions by which several sides of life are affected' (Tawney, 1964, 60).

I have stressed the need for more black teachers. Yet there is an equally urgent need for more black teacher educators, local education authority advisers, headteachers and deputy heads. The debate about positive discrimination is concerned with power sharing. Unfortunately, however, those in power invariably use their positions to advocate, rather than practise, the principle. The elected members tell the officers, the officers tell the headteachers, the headteachers tell the deputy heads, the deputy heads tell their staff that the vacant scale 1 post ought to be filled by a black teacher. It is not surprising, therefore, that the teacher in the classroom is disturbed by the obvious double standards that are being applied. The spokespersons for positive discrimination who have the power and influence to implement policy must find a way of sharing power *at their own level*.

COURSE CONTENT AND DESIGN

Provision is as important an issue as that of access. 'The evidence we have received from all sources', claimed the Rampton Report, 'presents an overwhelming picture of the failure of teacher training institutions to prepare teachers for their role in a multiracial society' (Department of Education and Science, 1981, 60). The same stance was taken by the recent report on racial disadvantage, issued by the House of Commons Home Affairs Committee in the same year, which stated that 'it is no longer acceptable to wait for the complex administrative structure of teacher training to come to terms in its own good time with the challenge presented by the multiracial classroom' (House of Commons, 1981a, para. 138). Progess in teacher education is slow. It needs to be speeded up.

A survey carried out in 1979 by Ray Giles and Derek Cherrington, in all colleges of higher education, polytechnics and universities providing teacher education in the United Kingdom, offers some useful information about the kinds of courses dealing with multicultural education. There were, Giles and Cherrington found, two basic approaches for the inclusion of multicultural education into the curricula of various programmes for teacher education. Either multicultural education was offered as a separate course of study (for example, as part of the programme for the B.Ed. or the Diploma in Higher Education or the Post Graduate Certificate in Education); or multicultural elements were included in some of the compulsory or optional courses in the various programmes. As far as content was concerned, there were three distinct strategies in evidence for both courses and elements of courses: those which helped to prepare teachers to understand and teach about Britain as a multicultural society; those which were presented to help teachers and students develop special competencies for teaching in schools or classrooms with racially or culturally diverse pupil populations; and those designed to address the needs of special populations. That last category would include topics such as English as a second language and mother-tongue teaching (Cherrington and Giles, 1981).

The information gathered by Giles and Cherrington is now, admittedly, somewhat dated and they themselves felt that the number of offerings within teacher education might well be expected to grow. Nevertheless, their criticisms still hold. Existing provision within teacher education for multicultural education remains insufficient. Moreover, where it exists, it tends to present multicultural education as an approach for dealing with a problem, rather than an educational concept valid for all pupils in a multicultural society:

In the relatively few teacher training institutions which have responded to the challenge of multicultural classrooms by offering specialist courses, most titles suggest that the 'problem' lies with the school children, rather than in the severely limited capacity or willingness of either the schools or most teachers to respond to a new situation . . . The entire school curriculum is culturally biased. What needs to be pointed out is that the history of Britain is one of interaction with many other peoples, and that British culture in all its forms has borrowed from and been influenced by other cultures from the earliest recorded history. This should be emphasised in the subject matter of every course taught in British schools. Only by helping teachers to become aware of, and to convey this perspective to all pupils, will the present bias which reinforces prejudice and racial discrimination be eliminated. (Cherrington and Giles, 1981, 82–3)

In stressing the historical dimension of the educational task, Giles and Cherrington are not suggesting that all teachers should become teachers of history, but that all student teachers should be made aware of the cultural complexity of British history and helped to relate this cultural complexity to their own subject specialisms and their own work in the classroom.

A joint working party of the former Community Relations

Commission and the Association of Teachers in Colleges and Departments of Education (a predecessor of the National Association of Teachers in Further and Higher Education) spelt out in greater detail the kind of informational input that ought to comprise a basic core component of all initial teacher education courses:

  (i) Why the postwar migration to this country from the Caribbean and the Indian sub-continent took place – put in perspective by also considering earlier migrations, e.g. the Jews, and the situation in other West European countries, e.g. France, Holland, West Germany.
 (ii) The impact of this migration on British society and politics since the war, the situation created by discrimination in housing and employment, the official agencies set up to deal with this and an estimate of their effectiveness.
(iii) The minority communities themselves, their religions, where they come from, how their life overseas differed from the situation here, how they have adapted, how they bring up their children, what this means for the teacher of these children, how the young black and brown British see this society, their future prospects.
 (iv) Prejudice, discrimination and racialism – the psychological and sociological explanations for prejudiced feelings and prejudiced behaviour, effect on children's learning and motivation in school of growing up in an environment where they are considered inferior.
  (v) The school in the community – how far does the school relate to the needs and values of the community it serves, how can the life of the particular community find expression in the organisation of the school, how far can teachers be expected to know and understand the community whose children they educate. (Commission for Racial Equality, 1978)

This checklist is not without its problems. In the second category, for example, there is no mention of racially discriminatory practices within education; an unfortunate omission given that housing and employment are singled out for special treatment. Nor, in the third category, is any sense of complex development, tension and conflict within particular minority communities conveyed. Moreover, since the working party pre-dated the 1981 British Nationality Act, there is no mention of this legislation, the implications of which should be fully understood by all teachers. The adoption on teacher education courses throughout the country of a core element of this kind, suitably updated with information from more recent studies of black people in Britain (such as that by Peter Fryer, 1984), would, nevertheless, still represent a highly significant advance.

Information, however, is not enough. Teachers' attitudes greatly influence what, and how, pupils learn. It is essential, therefore, that in any teacher education programme the affective dimension of multicultural education is taken seriously. For many students the subject of race and community relations evokes strong feelings. Ways must be found of helping all students to confront their own prejudices. A racism awareness component of some kind should be compulsory for all student teachers. Their prejudicial attitudes, conscious or otherwise, could have a disastrous effect on their future pupils. Every effort must be made to enable student teachers to analyse critically their own assumptions in this area and to develop alternative perspectives. Contact with members of ethnic minority groups is one way of breaking down stereotypes. In itself, though, this contact is not sufficient. There can be no substitute for self-appraisal and a rigorous analysis of the principles underlying one's own practice.

This raises the vexed question of how to assess affective learning of this kind. Many would see any attempt at such assessment as an infringement upon the personal liberty of the student. However, the danger of teachers entering the classroom with consciously held racist views or unexplored, implicitly racist values has been stressed repeatedly. Institutions of higher education which are responsible for initial teacher education cannot avoid the responsibility of monitoring their students' attitudes in this important area. The main criteria in any such assessment should be whether or not the student is willing and able to explore honestly his own attitudes and the assumptions underlying these attitudes. Where explicitly racist views are repeatedly expressed, the student's evident unsuitability for the teaching profession must be acknowledged. The instances in which this would be necessary are, I think, rare. The real danger is from the unexplored assumptions of those teachers who have never thought of themselves as holding racist views, but whose initial teacher education never allowed them the opportunity of exploring the implications of their own thinking. If this danger is to be averted in the future, much greater emphasis must be given on initial teacher education courses to raising students' awareness of racism as an issue which affects their own lives and shapes their own thinking.

Emphasis must also be placed on the education of the teacher educators. The cynicism and evasiveness of the following comment (taken from the responses to a questionnaire distributed as part of an in-service education initiative within an institution responsible for teacher education) by a lecturer working on initial teacher education courses is not uncommon: 'No radical changes envisaged. Quite frankly I think the whole question of multicultural education has been blown up out of all proportion and represents just one more of the passing phases to which "education" seems to be subject.' Clearly, until teacher educators are shaken out of this torpor, there can be little hope of any change, radical or otherwise. The recruitment of more black lecturers, although highly desirable in itself, is no solution to this problem. The intransigence and, in some cases, mental laziness of those who see no reason for change will still lead to inaction regardless of such recruitments. Nor is it enough (although, again, desirable) for the Department of Education and Science to produce, as the Home Affairs Committee recommended, 'a programme for training those intended to train teachers in multicultural education' (House of Commons, 1981b, 62). For those who stand in most need of such a programme would be least likely to attend it. More effective would be the exertion of outside pressure on teacher educators to revise existing courses and develop new ones that equipped all students to teach in a multicultural society. Validating bodies in the public and independent sectors have an important part to play in this respect. They should, as the Commission for Racial Equality's Advisory Group on Teacher Education has suggested, 'ensure that all teacher education courses give due consideration to the multicultural nature of British society' (Commission for Racial Equality, 1983, 78). (The discussion paper issued by the Council for National Academic Awards (1983) is to be welcomed as a step in this direction.) If pressure of this kind were put on teacher educators, they would have little option but to familiarize themselves with the issues and revise their courses accordingly. In-service education initiatives taken by the Department of Education and Science might then have some impact.

I have used the term 'teacher education' in this context, rather than the increasingly popular 'teacher training', because the former expresses the preoccupation with values, attitudes and awareness that is central to multicultural education. Teacher education must grasp firmly Paulo Freire's claim that 'It is not possible to teach methods without problematizing the whole structure in which these methods will be used' (Freire, 1976, 155). For education, by definition, challenges our existing knowledge, our preconceptions, and the ways in which we use the skills we have already acquired and are still acquiring. It is a mode of critical and reflective practice. Multicultural education can never be reduced to a set of procedures. It is the form our questions take when they focus upon a crucial aspect of equality of opportunity and access.

IN-SERVICE EDUCATION

Although initial teacher education is an extremely important area of concern, new entrants to the teaching profession amount, each year, to little more than 2.5 per cent of the total teaching force. Initial teacher education courses can, therefore, make only a limited impact overall. Adequate in-service provision is required if the necessary inroads are to be made into the thinking and practice of serving teachers. This is a particularly urgent requirement, given that most practising teachers had no opportunity in their pre-service education to consider issues relating to multicultural education.

Unfortunately, as the Department of Education and Science enquiry on 'In-Service Teacher Education in a Multi-Racial Society' has shown, in-service provision in the area of multicultural education is fragmentary and incomplete. Indeed, it is non-existent in many local education authorities and in none, according to John Eggleston and his colleagues who conducted the enquiry, is it wholly adequate. Even in those areas where relevant courses are being run teachers may not be aware of it, since 'awareness of any course depends upon the almost random chance of information reaching the school, reaching the noticeboard and being read by staff concerned' (Eggleston, Dunn and Purewal, 1981, 336). Thus, in spite of a heavy demand for in-service courses relating to the education of pupils for a multicultural society, recruitment is often very poor.

In addition to highlighting the need for improving the communicative networks in schools, Eggleston and his team also argued for a 'more coherent and comprehensive organis-ation of provision on national and regional lines' (ibid., 359). Without some such overall planning it is difficult to see how any continuity within in-service education can be achieved. Such continuity is important if teachers attending courses of this kind are to receive the recognition and accreditation due to them. A clearly defined structure of in-service provision, possibly with specified levels of achievement, would offer teachers the opportunity of developing a theoretical and practical understanding of what is involved in educating pupils for life in a multicultural society.

This stress on the importance of the in-service *course* should not be taken to imply an undervaluing of the kind of school-based evaluative work advocated in the previous chapter. If school-focused in-service work is to prove effective, it must include both an off-site and an on-site element. In order to develop professionally teachers need to be able to stand back from the immediate concerns of schooling, to adopt a theoretical perspective, to talk with colleagues from other schools and sectors of the education service, to read. Off-site in-service provision can offer them the opportunity of partici-pating in these more reflective activities. They also need to be able to extend their skills and insights in relation to their own immediate situation in schools. On-site in-service provision can make an important contribution in this area.

The problem is, of course, to ensure that these two kinds of provision complement one another. This problem is exacer-bated, as Ted Wragg's recent review of research in teacher education has shown, by the fact that we know very little about how in-service courses influence classroom teaching (Wragg, 1982, 75). We do know, however, that the impact of such courses is likely to be greater in those schools where there is a clearly defined pattern of on-site provision and where a real effort is made by the headteacher and senior staff to feed into the work of the school the insights gained by teachers attending in-service courses. The careful targeting of courses to meet the needs of particular groups of teachers in specific areas is also likely to result, not only in increased recruitment for such courses, but in more practically orientated outcomes.

Certain kinds of publications can help to bridge the gap between the practical demands of on-site in-service work and the more general concerns of the traditional off-site course. School-based evaluations, records of work in progress and local working party reports can help to inform and extend discussions within individual schools. The significance of this kind of literature for the purposes of in-service education is that it creates valuable links, facilitating dialogue between teachers and strengthening existing networks. Collections of papers by practising teachers based in a single school (see, for example, Talk Workshop Group, 1982) and discussion documents produced by teachers committed to a particular classroom approach (for example, Rudduck, 1979), although local in origin, address a broad constituency. Documents of this kind help to keep open the channels of communication between schools and the wider educational context and to ensure that the dialogue is a two-way one.

In doing so they perform an extremely useful function. For there can be no effective coordination of the various strands of in-service education provision until teachers, local education authority advisers, lecturers in institutions of higher education and members of Her Majesty's Inspectorate come together to decide on the kinds of questions that should form the basis of a nationwide in-service programme in multicultural education. Clearly, there would be regional variations in the pattern of provision and it might be appropriate to think in terms of a two-tiered system, with the regions responding to local needs and national support for a common core of professional concerns. Without some such system, however, in-service education in the area of multicultural education will rely upon self-help and isolated initiatives, which, regardless of their quality, can provide little more than a patchwork quilt of provision.

The kinds of questions on which a coordinated programme of this kind should be based have been a major concern throughout this book. Such questions can, I believe, be expressed in practical terms, although their eventual resolution must also be at a high level of generality. The following may serve as an example of what I have in mind:

– What aspects of your school conflict with the pupils'

backgrounds and previous experience? Is this conflict inevitable or could it be partially resolved?
- Where are the growth points in multicultural education within your own school or area? How could you build on these?
- How do you as an individual teacher respond to incidents of racist behaviour or abuse involving pupils and/or colleagues? Could the school support you more fully in this respect?
- What procedures do you adopt when discussing controversial issues with pupils? Do your colleagues adopt the same procedures?
- Is the language you use in your classroom always understood by your pupils? How important do you think it is to relate the language you use to your pupils' experience?
- How could you begin to examine more closely the language of the pupils you teach?
- Are there any local community groups with which your school might usefully make contact? Are there any existing contacts between the school and community that you, as an individual teacher, might utilize?
- How do you know when a pupil, involved in advanced work, still requires help in the more difficult aspects of language use in your subject?

These are examples only. Much more extensive documentation is available from schools and local education authorities (see, for example, Inner London Education Authority, 1981; and Brent London Borough, 1983). It should be noted, however, that all these questions assume some knowledge concerning the cultural and linguistic diversity of British society. This is one of the areas in which off-site in-service education has an important contribution to make. Teachers need to *know*. It should also be noted that these questions assume an anti-racist stance by the teacher. Such a stance is, I believe, a moral imperative for all those involved in the formulation of an in-service education programme within the area of multicultural education. It involves close and equal cooperation between the school, the wider educational context and all sections of the local community. Teachers need to *connect*.

To sum up. Teacher education is in a chronic state of insecurity. The dictates of local and central government have only served to intensify this uncertainty. Wider access to teacher education should be a central concern of all those committed to the notion of equal opportunity. Yet access is not the only issue. The curriculum of initial teacher education needs to be reviewed, revised and updated. Those involved in in-service education, both as teachers and as teacher educators, need to develop a coordinated system by means of which all teachers can think through the issues relating to multicultural education, which for all its compromises has a vital part to play in the reconstruction of a genuinely comprehensive education system. Whether, in retrospect, it will be seen to have fulfilled this role will depend to a great extent on the capacity of practising teachers to respond to those of its critics who are impatient for justice.

Bibliography

AFFOR (1982), *Talking Chalk: Black Pupils, Parents and Teachers Speak about Education* (AFFOR, 173 Lozells Road, Lozells, Birmingham B19 1RN)

Afro-Caribbean Education Resource Project (1982), *School Policy Group: ACER Follow-up to the Rampton Report* (275 Kennington Lane, London SE11 5QZ)

Afro-Caribbean Education Resource Project (undated), *Links Between School and Community: Comments on the Rampton Report* (275 Kennington Lane, London SE11 5QZ)

Alexander, Z. and Dewjee, A. (eds) (1984), *Wonderful Adventures of Mrs Seacole in Many Lands*, Falling Wall Press.

Allison, B. (1981), 'Art Education and Teaching about the Art of Asia, Africa and Latin America', *Educational Journal* (Commission for Racial Equality), 3, 3 (July), pp. 6–8.

Armstrong, M. (1980), *Closely Observed Children*, Writers and Readers/ Chameleon

Armstrong, M. (1981), 'The Case of Louise and the Painting of Landscape', in J. Nixon (ed.), pp. 15–36

Austin, H. and Garrison, L. (1978), 'Resources for Black Pupils', *Times Educational Supplement*, 24 February

Bagley, C. and Coard, B. (1975), 'Cultural Knowledge and Rejection of Ethnic Identity in West Indian Children in London', in G. Verma and C. Bagley (eds), pp. 322–31

Barnes, J. and Lucas, H. (1975), 'Positive Discrimination in Education', in J. Barnes (ed.), *Education priority*, vol, 3, HMSO

Berkshire Royal County (1982) *A Paper for Discussion*, Summer (Department of Education, Royal County of Berkshire, Shire Hall, Shinfield Park, Reading RG2 9XE)

Berry, J. (1981), *Fractured Circles*, New Beacon Books

Berry, J. (1982), *Lucy's Letters and Loving*, New Beacon Books

Birley High School (1980), *Multi-cultural Education in the 1980's*, Report of a working party of teachers at Birley High School, Chichester Road, Hulme, Manchester M15 5FU, May

Birmingham Education Department (1982), *Recognising Racism* (available in filmstrip or slideset from Multicultural Support Services, Bordesley Centre, Stratford Road, Birmingham B11 1AR)

Black Peoples Progressive Association (1978), *Cause for Concern: West Indian Pupils in Redbridge*, Redbridge Community Relations Council, (Methodist Church Hall, Ilford Lane, Ilford, Essex)

Black Pressure Group on Education (1983), *Resolution* (West Green Community Centre, Stanley road, Tottenham, London N5), 13 February

Black Pressure Group on Education (1984), Report on the conference entitled 'Racism in Schools: Ways Forward for Haringey' held at Haringey Teachers' Centre on Saturday, 10 March 1984 (West Green Community Centre, Stanley Road, Tottenham, London N5)

Boateng, P. (1984) 'The Police, the Community and Accountability', in J. Benyon (ed.), *Scarman and After*, Pergamon Press, pp. 152–9

Brathwaite, E. (1973), *The Arrivants: a New World Trilogy*, Oxford University Press

Brent London Borough (1982), *Report No. 44/82 of the Director of Education*, Education Committee

Brent London Borough (1983), *Education for a Multicultural Democracy*, 2, Education Committee

Brent Teachers' Association (1980), *Multicultural Education in Brent Schools* (Director of Education, London Borough of Brent, Chesterfield House, 9 Park Lane, Wembley, Middlesex)

British Association for Counselling (1979), *Counselling: Definition of Terms*

Brookes, M. (1980), 'The Mother Tongue Issue in Britain: Cultural Diversity or Control?', *British Journal of Sociology of Education*, 1, 3

Carby, H. (1982), 'Schooling in Babylon', in Centre for Contemporary Cultural Studies, pp. 183–211

Centre for Contemporary Cultural Studies (1982), *The Empire Strikes Back: Race and Racism in 70's Britain*, Hutchinson

Centre for World Development Education (1979), *The Changing World and R.E.* (128 Buckingham Palace Road, London SW1)

Cherrington, D. and Giles, R. (1981), 'Present Provision in initial Training', in M. Craft (ed.), pp. 75–85

Claire, H. (1983), ' "Memories" – A Project for the Multi-cultural Classroom', *Multi-ethnic Education Review* (ILEA, Room 468, County Hall, London SE1 7PB), 2, 1 (Winter/Spring), pp. 12–15

Clarke, J., Critcher, C. and Johnson, R. (eds) (1979), *Working Class Culture: Studies in History and Theory*, Hutchinson

Cleveland, R. (1983), *A Study of the Relationship Between Some Afro-Caribbean Supplementary Schools and the State System*, unpublished study submitted for the degree of In-Service, B.Ed. (hons), Middlesex Polytechnic

Coard, B. (1971), *How the West Indian Child is made Educationally Sub-normal in the British School System: The Scandal of the Black Child in Schools in Britain*, New Beacon Books

Cohen, L. and Manion, L. (1983), *Multicultural Classrooms*, Croom Helm

Coleraine Boys' Secondary School (undated), 'Scheme of Work: Integrated Studies'

Collicot, S. (1980), 'Strange Feelings', *Child Education*, December, p. 23

Commission for Racial Equality (1978), *Teacher Education for a Multicultural Society*, first published jointly by the Community Relations Commission and the Association of Teachers in Colleges and Departments of Education, 1974

Commission for Racial Equality (1980), 'Multicultural Education for All: A Practical Example', *Educational Journal*, 2, 2 (April)

Commission for Racial Equality (1983), *Multicultural Britain: The Preparation of Teachers*, Advisory group on teacher education, January (first draft)

Commonwealth Immigrants Advisory Council (1964), *Report*, Cmnd 2266, HMSO

Conservative Party (1979), 'The Conservative Manifesto 1979', in *The Times Guide to the House of Commons*, Times Books

Council for National Academic Awards (1983), *Multicultural Education: Discussion Paper*, Education Committee working group on multicultural education, June

Craft, M. (ed.) (1981), *Teaching in a Multicultural Society: The Task for Teacher Education*, Falmer Press

Crellin, C.T. (1982), 'Special Access Link Course', *Education Journal* (Commission for Racial Equality), 4, 1 (March), p. 15

Cupitt, D. (1979), *Explorations in Theology 6*, SCM Press

Daily Mirror (1965), 'No Coloureds Said the Chinese Waiter', 23 April, included in the original pack of materials published as part of the Programme of Research in the Problems and Effects of Teaching about Race Relations, Centre for Applied Research in Education, University of East Anglia

Department of Education and Science (1965), *The Education of Immigrants*, Circular 7/65, June

Department of Education and Science (1975), *A Language for Life*, The Bullock Report, HMSO

Department of Education and Science (1977), *A New Partnership for Our Schools*, The Taylor Report, HMSO

Department of Education and Science (1978), Letter to CEO's, Avon, Bedfordshire, Birmingham, Haringey, ILEA, Leicestershire, and Manchester, 2 August, in National Association of Teachers in Further and Higher Education (1979), *Further and Teacher*

Education in a Multicultural Society, pp. 95–7

Department of Education and Science (1980), *Access Courses to Higher Education*, DES conference report (conference held at the Commonwealth Institute, Kensington High Street, London, 17–18 November 1980)

Department of Education and Science (1981), *West Indian Children in Our Schools*, The Rampton Report, interim report of the committee of inquiry into the education of children from ethnic minority groups, HMSO

Department of Education and Science (1983), *Teaching Quality*, White Paper, HMSO

Department of Education and Science (1984a), *Parental Influence at School*, Green Paper, HMSO

Department of Education and Science (1984b), *Final Report of the Committee of Inquiry into the Education of Children from Ethnic Minority Groups*, The Swann Report, forthcoming, HMSO

Dhondy, F. (1973), 'Overtly Political Focus', *Times Educational Supplement*, 2 November

Dhondy, F. (1982), 'The Black Explosion in British Schools', in F. Dhondy, B. Beese and L. Hassan, *The Black Explosion in British Schools*, Race Today Publications, pp. 43–52 (165 Railton Road, London SE24 0LU)

Dixon, B. (1977), *Catching Them Young*, Pluto Press

Dodgson, E. (1982), 'Exploring Social Issues', in J. Nixon (ed.) (1982), pp. 97–112

Dodgson, E. (1984), *Motherland: West Indian Women to Britain in the 1950s*, Heinemann

Dodgson, P. and Stewart, D. (1981), 'Multiculturalism or Anti-racist Teaching: A Question of Alternatives', *Multiracial Education*, 9, 3, pp. 2–9

Doughty, P., Pearce, J. and Thornton, G. (1971), *Language in Use*, Edward Arnold

Du Bois, W.E.B. (1975), *The Education of Black People: Ten Critiques 1906–1960*, Monthly Review Press

Edwards, V.K. (1979), *The West Indian Language Issue in British Schools*, Routledge & Kegan Paul

Eggleston, J., Dunn, D.K. and Purewal, A. (1981), *In-service Teacher Education in a Multiracial Society*, University of Keele, April

Emecheta, B. (1974), *Second-class Citizen*, Fontana

Enright, L. (1981), 'The Diary of a Classroom', in Nixon (ed.), pp. 37–51

Ezard, J. (1983), *The Guardian*, 7 January

File, N. and Power, C. (1981), *Black Settlers in Britain 1555–1958*, Heinemann

Francis, M. (1982), 'We Decided to Lie About Our Ages: Anti-racism in the Primary School', *Teaching London Kids*, 21, pp. 16–20 (TLK, 20 Durham Road, London SW20)

Freire, P. (1976), *Education: The Practice of Freedom*, Writers and Readers

Fryer, P. (1984), *Staying Power: The History of Black People in Britain*, Pluto Press

Fyson, N.L. and Greenhill, S. (1979), *New Commonwealth Immigrants*, Macmillan

Gibbes, N. (1980), *West Indian Teachers Speak Out*, Caribbean Teachers Association and Lewisham Community Relation Committee

Gill, D. (1982), *Geography and the Young School Leaver: A Critique*, Centre for Multicultural Education, University of London, Working Paper No. 2

Guardian (1978), 'Old-fashioned Learning by Rote Pays Off', 20 February

Hall, S. (1980), 'Teaching Race', *Multiracial Education*, 9, 1 (Autumn), pp. 3–13

Halsey, A.H. (1977), 'Whatever Happened to Positive Discrimination?', in R. Raggatt and M. Evans, *The Political Context*, The Open University, Faculty of Education Studies, Urban Education 3, Ward Lock, pp. 140–5

Hamblin, D. (1974), *The Teacher and Counselling*, Blackwell

Hargreaves, D.H. (1982), *The Challenge for the Comprehensive School: Culture, Curriculum and Community*, Routledge & Kegan Paul

Harlen, W. (ed.) (1978), *Evaluation and the Teacher's Role*, Schools Council Research Studies, Macmillan

Hatcher, R. (1983), 'The Construction of World Studies', *Multiracial Education*, 11, 1 (Winter), pp. 23–36

Hemmings, R. (1980a), 'Multi-ethnic Mathematics: Part 1 Primary', *New Approaches in Multiracial Education*, 8, 3 (Summer), pp. 1–4

Hemmings, R. (1980b), 'Multi-ethnic Mathematics: Part 2 Secondary', *Multiracial Education*, 9, 1 (Autumn), pp. 29–38

Hicks, D. (1979), 'Two Sides of the Same Coin: An Exploration of Links Between Multicultural Education and Development Education', *New Approaches to Multiracial Education*, 7, 2 (Spring), pp. 1–5

Hicks, D. (1980), *Bias in Geography Textbooks: Images of the Third World and Multi-ethnic Education*, Centre for Multicultural Education, University of London, Working Paper No. 1

Hinds, D. (1966), *Journey to an Illusion: The West Indian in Britain*, Heinemann

Hiro, D. (1973), *Black British, White British*, Penguin

Houlton, D. (1983), 'Responding to Diversity', in Schools Council, *Teaching in a Culturally Diverse Society: Papers from a National Conference* (October), pp. 6–16 (Information Centre, Schools Council, Newcombe House, 45 Notting Hill Gate, London W11 3JB)

Houlton, D. and Willey, R. (1983), *Supporting Children's Bilingualism*, Longman

House of Commons (1981a), *Racial Disadvantage*, 5th Report from the Home Affairs Committee, vol. 1, HMSO

House of Commons (1981b), *Racial Disadvantage*, 5th Report from the Home Affairs Committee, vol. 4 (memorandum submitted by the National Association of Teachers in Further and Higher Education), HMSO

Hoyle, P. (1983), 'Solids, liquids and language', in Issues in Race and Education No. 39, *Learning and Language: ESL in the Mainstream Classroom*, pp. 12–13 (11 Carleton Gardens, Brecknock Road, N19 5AQ)

Inner London Education Authority (1978), *Lambeth Whole School Project*, Education Committee – Further and Higher Education Sub-Committee and Schools Sub-Committee, Report by Education Officer, 3 May

Inner London Education Authority (1981), *Education in a Multi-ethnic: An Aide-memoire for the Inspectorate* (County Hall, London SE1 7PB)

Inner London Education Authority (1983), *Race, Sex and Class*
  (1) 'Achievement in Schools'
  (2) 'Multi-ethnic Education in Schools'
  (3) 'A Policy for Equality: Race'
  (4) 'Anti-racist Statement and Guidelines'
  (5) 'Multi-ethnic Education in Further, Higher and Community Education' (County Hall, London SE1 7PB)

Institute of Race Relations (1982), *Book 1 Roots of Racism, Book 2 Patterns of Racism* (247/9 Pentonville Road, London N1 9NG)

Issues in Race and Education (1982), *Parents Teachers Communities*, No. 37 (11 Carleton Gardens, Brecknock Road, London N19 5AQ) (Autumn)

Jackson, D. (1981), 'Food for Thought', in J. Nixon (ed.), pp. 52–60

James, A. and Jeffcoate, R. (eds) (1981), *The School in the Multicultural Society*, Harper & Row

James, M. and Ebbutt, D. (1981), 'Problems and Potentials', in J. Nixon (ed.), pp. 81–95

Jeffcoate, R. (1979), *Positive Image: Towards a Multiracial Curriculum*, Writers and Readers/Chameleon

Jeffcoate, R. (1984), *Ethnic Minorities and Education*, Harper & Row

Jenkins, R. (1966), *Address Given by the Home Secretary to a Meeting of Voluntary Liaison Committees*

Johnson, R. (1979), ' "Really Useful Knowledge": Radical Education and Working Class Culture', in J. Clarke, C. Critcher and R. Johnson (eds), pp. 75–102

Jones, C. (1977), *Immigration and Social Policy in Britain*, Tavistock

Jones, C. and Klein, G. (1980), *Assessing Children's Books for a Multi-ethnic Society*, Centre for Urban Educational Studies, ILEA

Kapo, R. (1981), *A Savage Culture: Racism – A Black British View*, Quartet Books

Katz, J. (1978), *White Awareness: Handbook for anti-racism Training*,

University of Oklahoma Press

Keddie, N. (ed.) (1973), *Tinker, Tailor . . . : The Myth of Cultural Deprivation*, Penguin

Killian, L. (1981), *Affirmative Action and Protective Discrimination: A Comparison of the United States and India*, Centre for Multicultural Education, University of London Institute of Education, Occasional Paper No. 3

Klein, G. (1981), 'Kids, Schools and Libraries', *Education Journal* (Commission for Racial Equality), 3, 2 (March), pp. 3–4

Klein, G. (1982), *Resources for Multicultural Education*, Schools Council

Labov, W. (1973), 'The Logic of Nonstandard English', in N. Keddie, pp. 21–66

Lago, C. (1981), 'Cross-cultural Counselling: Some Developments, Thoughts and Hypotheses', *New Community*, 9, 1 (Spring–Summer), pp. 59–63

Lago, C. and Ball, R. (1983), 'The Almost Impossible Task: Helping in a Multi-cultural Context', *Multiracial Education*, 11, 2 (Spring), pp. 39–50

Lamming, G. (1980), *The Emigrants*, Allison & Busby (first published in Great Britain 1954)

Language and Class Workshop (1974), Number 1 (February) (available from 41a Muswell Hill, London N10)

Language in the Multicultural Primary Classroom (1982), 'Using Children's Knowledge as a Resource and Liaising With a Colleague', *Broadsheet 2*, Work in Progress (October), Schools Council

Levine, J. (1983), ' "Going Back" to the Mainstream', in Issues in Race and Education No. 39, *Learning and Language: ESL in the Mainstream Classroom*, pp. 1–3 (11 Carleton Gardens, Brecknock Road, London N19 5AQ)

Linguistic Minorities Project (1983), *Linguistic Minorities in Britain* (Institute of Education, University of London, 18 Woburn Square, London WC1R 0NS)

Little, A. and Willey, R. (1981), *Multi-ethnic Education: The Way Forward*, Schools Council Pamphlet 18

Lynch, J. (ed.) (1981), *Teaching in the Multi-cultural School*, Ward Lock

Lynch, J. (1983a), *The Multicultural Curriculum*, Batsford

Lynch, J. (1983b), 'Teaching in a Culturally Diverse Society', in Schools Council, *Teaching in a Culturally Diverse Society: Papers from a National Conference* (October), pp. 17–23 (Information Centre, Schools Council, Newcombe House, 45 Notting Hill Gate, London W11 3JB)

Miles, R. (1982), *Racism and Migrant Labour*, Routledge & Kegan Paul

Milner, D. (1975), *Children and Race*, Penguin

Moltmann, J. (1981), *The Trinity and the Kingdom of God*, SCM Press (first published in Germany 1980)

Mullard, C. (1980), *Racism in Society and Schools: History, Policy and*

Practice, Centre for Multicultural Education, University of London Institute of Education, Occasional Paper No. 1

Nagra, J.S. (1981/2), 'Asian Supplementary Schools: A Case Study of Coventry', *New Community*, 9, 3, pp. 431–6

National Union of Teachers (1979), *In Black and White: Guidelines for Teachers on Racial Stereotyping in Textbooks and Learning Materials*

Neil, A. (1982), 'In loco parentis', in Issues in Race and Education No. 37, *Parents Teachers Communities*, pp. 6–7 (Autumn) (11 Carleton Gardens, Brecknock Road, N19 5AQ)

Nias, J. (1984), *A More Distant Drummer: Teacher Development as the Development of Self*, mimeo (Cambridge Institute of Education, Shaftesbury Road, Cambridge CB2 2BX)

Nichols, G. (1983), *I is a long-memoried woman*, Caribbean Cultural International (Karnak House, 300 Westbourne Park Road, London W11 1EH)

Nixon, J. (ed.) (1981), *A Teachers' Guide to Action Research*, Grant McIntyre

Nixon, J. (1981/2), 'Multi-ethnic Education in Inner London', *New Community*, 9, 3, pp. 381–98

Nixon, J. (ed.) (1982a), *Drama and the Whole Curriculum*, Hutchinson

Nixon, J. (1982b), 'Strategy C Case Studies', in L. Stenhouse et al., pp. 185–233

Nixon, J. and Verrier, R. (1979), 'A Case Study of a Collaborative In-service Relationship', *Cambridge Journal of Education*, 9, 2 and 3, pp. 121–7

North Westminster Community School (1982), *Towards a Multi-cultural Philosophy* (a policy statement agreed by the whole staff at North Westminster Community School, Penfold Street, London NW1)

Office of Population Censuses and Surveys (1977), *Demographic Review*, HMSO

Patterson, S. (1965), *Dark Strangers: A Study of West Indians in London*, Penguin (first published by Tavistock 1963)

Policy Studies Institute (1983), *Police and People in London*
  (1) 'A Survey of Londoners', D.J. Smith
  (2) 'A Group of Young Black People', S. Small
  (3) 'A Survey of Police Officers', D.J. Smith
  (4) 'The Police in Action', D.J. Smith and J. Gray

Pollack, M. (1972), 'A Suggested Black Studies Syllabus', *Teachers against Racism*, No. 7, pp. 10–11

Quintin Kynaston School (1980), *Quintin Kynaston Policy on Racist Behaviour: A Statement for the Staff Handbook* (Quintin Kynaston School, Marlborough Hill, London NW8 0NL)

Quintin Kynaston School (1982), 'Quintin Kynaston Policy on Racist Behaviour', in ILEA Multi-Ethnic Inspectorate, *Anti-Racist Policies* (NB This QK statement differs slightly from the earlier version)

Race and Immigration (1983), *The Runnymede Trust Bulletin*, No. 159 (September)

Rack, P. (1978), *In Working With Asian Young People*, National Association for Asian Youth

Ranson, P. (1983), 'Avoiding Discrimination in Texts and Reading Materials: An Examination of Books in a Primary School', in C. Adelman and others, *A Fair Hearing for All*, Bulmershe Research Publication No. 2 (Bulmershe College of Higher Education, Earley, Reading RG6 1HY), pp. 34–44

Reading through Understanding (1978), *Make-a-story* (for 5–8 year olds), *Share-a-story* (for 5–11 year olds), *Explore-a-story* (for 9–13 year olds), Centre for Urban Education Studies (Robert Montefiore Building, Underwood Road, London E1)

Riley, K. (1982), 'Policing the Police, Teaching the Teachers: Scarman, Rampton and MP's Read the Riot Lessons', *Multiracial Education*, 10, 2 (Spring), pp. 3–10

Rogers, B. (1980), *Race: No Peace Without Justice*, World Council of Churches, Geneva

Rogers, C. (1951), *Client Centred Therapy*, Houghton Mifflin

Rosen, H. and Burgess, T. (1980), *Languages and Dialects of London School Children*, Ward Lock

Rosendale Junior School (1981), *Multi-cultural Policy Document*, October, (Croxted Road, West Dulwich, London SE21)

Ruddell, D. (1983), 'Racism Awareness: An Approach for Schools', *Multiracial Education*, 11, 1 (Winter), pp. 3–9

Rudduck, J. (ed.) (1979), *Learning to Teach Through Discussion*, Centre for Applied Research in Education, University of Norwich

Runnymede Trust and Radical Statistics Race Group (1980), *Britain's Black Population*, Heinemann

Scarman (1982), *The Brixton Disorders 10–12 April 1981*, The Scarman Report, Penguin (first published by HMSO 1981)

Schools Council (1977), *Journeys into Religion*, Hart-Davis

Schools Council (1981), *Examining in a Multi-cultural Society*, December, A report of the conference held at the Schools Council, 25 September

Scobie, E. (1972), *Black Britannia: A History of Blacks in Britain*, Johnson (Chicago)

Searle, C. (1973), *The Forsaken Lover: White Words and Black People*, Penguin

Searle, C. (1975), *Classrooms of Resistance*, Writers and Readers

Searle, C. (1983), 'A Common Language', *Race and Class*, 25, 2 (Autumn), pp. 65–74

Selvon, S. (1956), *The Lonely Londoners*, Alan Wingate (reissued by Longman in 1979)

Shipman, M. (1979), *In-school Evaluation*, Heinemann

Shyllon, F. (1974), *Black Slaves in Britain*, Oxford University Press

Shyllon, F. (1977), *Black People in Britain 1555–1833*, Oxford University Press

Sikes, P. (ed.) (1979), *Teaching about Race Relations*, National Association for Race Relations Teaching and Action Research (c/o Centre for Applied Research in Education, University of East Anglia, Norwich NR4 7TJ)

Simons, H. (1981), 'Conversation Piece: The Practice of Interviewing in Case Study Research', in C. Adelman (ed.), *Uttering, Muttering*, Grant McIntyre

Sivanandan, A. (1982), *A Different Hunger: Writings on Black Resistance*, Pluto Press

Smiddy, J. (1981), 'Creating a team', in J. Nixon (ed.), pp. 108–20

Smith, D.J. (1977), *Racial Disadvantage in Britain*, The PEP Report, Penguin

Stenhouse, L. (1975), *An Introduction to Curriculum Research and Development*, Heinemann

Stenhouse, L. (1983), *Authority, Education and Emancipation*, Heinemann

Stenhouse, L., Verma, G.K., Wild, R.D., and Nixon, J. (1982), *Teaching about Race Relations: Problems and Effects*, Routledge & Kegan Paul

Stone, M. (1981), *The Education of the Black Child in Britain: The Myth of Multiracial Education*, Fontana

Sutcliffe, D. (1982), *British Black English*, Blackwell

Talk Workshop Group (1982), *Becoming Our Own Experts* (available from ILEA English Centre, Sutherland Street, London SW1)

Tawney, R.H. (1964), *Equality*, Allen & Unwin (first published in 1931)

Tierney, J. (ed.) (1982), *Race, Migration and Schooling*, Holt Education

Times Educational Supplement (1982), 'A Multicultural Approach to History Teaching', 10 December

Tizard, B., Mortimore, J. and Burchell, B. (1981), *Involving Parents in Nursery and Infant Schools*, Grant McIntyre

Townsend, H. and Brittan, E. (1973), *Multiracial Education: Need and Innovation*, Schools Council Working Paper 50, Evans/Methuen Educational

Troyna, B. and Ball, W. (1983), 'Multicultural Education Policies: Are They Worth the Paper They're Written on?', *Times Educational Supplement*, 9 December, p. 20

Truax, C. and Carkhuff, R. (1967), *Towards Effective Counselling and Psychotherapy*, Aldine

Twitchin, J. and Demuth, C. (1981), *Multi-cultural Education: Views from the Classroom*, British Broadcasting Corporation

Verma, G. and Bagley, C. (eds) (1975), *Race and Education Across Cultures*, Heinemann

Walsall Metropolitan Borough (1982), *Education in a Multi-cultural Society: Curricular Implications*, Education Committee-Programme Sub-Committee, January

Williams, R. (1983), *Towards 2000*, Chatto & Windus/The Hogarth Press

Wohl, J. (1976), 'Interactional Psychotheraphy Issues: Questions and Reflections', in P. Pederson, W. Loner and J. Dragnus, *Counselling Across Cultures*, University of Hawaii, Honolulu

World History Project (1978), *Classroom Approaches to World History*, ILEA Learning Resources Centre (275 Kennington Lane, London SE11 5QZ)

Wragg, E.C. (1982), *A Review of Research in Teacher Education*, NFER/Nelson

Wright, D. (1983), 'A Portrait of Racism in Geography', *Education Journal* (Commission for Racial Equality), 5, 2, pp. 1–5

Wright, J. (1982), *Bilingualism in Education*, Issues in Race and Educaton (11 Carleton Gardens, Brecknock Road, London N19 5AQ)

Young, M.F.D. (ed.) (1971), *Knowledge and Control*, Collier-Macmillan

Zec, P. (1981), 'Multicultural Education: What Kind of Relativism is Possible?', in A. James and R. Jeffcoate (eds), pp. 29–44

Index